READ TO WORK

TRADE & INDUSTRY

ELLEN FRECHETTE

CAMBRIDGE ADULT EDUCATION
A Division of Simon & Schuster
Upper Saddle River, New Jersey

Author: **Ellen Frechette**
Series Editorial Consultant: Harriet Diamond, *President, Diamond Associates, Multifaceted Training and Development, Westfield NJ*

Reviewers:
Margaret Kirkpatrick, *Berkeley Adult School, Berkeley CA*
Jackie Anger, *Institute for Labor Studies & Research, Cranston RI*

Director, Editorial & Marketing, Adult Education: Diane Galen
Market Manager: Will Jarred
Assistant Market Manager: Donna Frasco
Editorial Development: Learning Unlimited, Inc.
Project Editors: Douglas Falk, Elena Petron
Editorial Assistant: Kathleen Kennedy
Production Director: Kurt Scherwatzky
Production Editor: John Roberts
Art Direction: Pat Smythe, Kenny Beck
Cover Art: Jim Finlayson
Interior Design & Electronic Page Production: Levavi & Levavi
Photo Research: Jenifer Hixson

Photo Credits: p. 6: Stock Boston; p. 15: Cary Wolinsky, Stock Boston; p. 22: Cary Wolinsky, Stock Boston; p. 33: Richard Hutchings, Photo Researchers; p. 41: Peter Vandermark, Stock Boston; p. 47: Lenny Nelson; p. 57: Scott and Gillian Aldrich; p. 65: Scott and Gillian Aldrich; p. 72: Bob Daemmrich, Stock Boston; p. 82: Scott and Gillian Aldrich; p. 90: WB Spunbarg, The Picture Cube; p. 97: Sarah Putman, The Picture Cube.

Printed in the United States of America
2 3 4 5 6 7 8 9 10   01 00 99 98

ISBN: 0-8359-4680-0

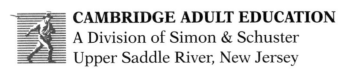

CAMBRIDGE ADULT EDUCATION
A Division of Simon & Schuster
Upper Saddle River, New Jersey

C O N T E N T S

T O   T H E   L E A R N E R

Welcome to the *Read To Work* series. The books in this series were written with you, the adult learner, in mind. Good reading skills are important in the world of work for these reasons:

 ◆ They may help you get the job you want.
 ◆ They will help you learn how to do your job well.
 ◆ They can help you get a better job.

The lessons in this book, *Read To Work: Trade and Industry,* will help you improve your reading skills. As you work through the lessons, you will also learn about jobs in different industries and in the skilled trades.

UNITS

Read To Work: Trade and Industry is divided into four units. Each unit covers different kinds of jobs. You can look at the **Contents** to see what fields and jobs are covered in this book.

LESSONS

Each unit contains at least 3 lessons. Each lesson teaches one reading skill and covers one kind of job. Here are some things to look for as you read each lesson:

Words to Know are words you will learn in the lessons. Look for the meaning of each new word to the left of what you are reading. You will also see a respelling of the words like this: *pronunciation* (proh-nun-see-AY-shuhn). This respelling will help you say the word correctly. There is a guide to help you with the respellings on page 101.

Job Focus describes the job in the lesson. It also tells you what types of skills are needed to do the job.

How It Works teaches you about the reading skill and how you can use it.

Readings include memos, pages from handbooks and manuals, posters, product guidelines, safety notices, and articles from company newsletters. If you look through this book, you will see that the reading passages look different from the rest of the lesson. They are examples of reading materials from the world of work.

Check Your Understanding questions can be multiple choice, short answer, or true/false. They will help you check that you understand the reading.

On the Job gives you a chance to read about real people as they do their jobs.

OTHER LEARNING AIDS

There are other learning aids at the back of the book. They are:

Respelling Guide: help with pronouncing words
Resources: where to get more information on the jobs in the book
Glossary: definitions of the Words to Know
Index: job names in the book
Answer Key: answers to *Check Your Understanding* and *Lesson Wrap-Up* questions

Now you are ready to begin using *Read To Work: Trade and Industry.* We hope that you will enjoy this book and learn from it.

⋅ Processing Occupations ⋅

The jobs you will focus on in Unit One are **Processing occupations** (ahk-yoo-PAY-shuns). Many steps are involved in the processes of making food, glass, fabric, and thousands of other products we use every day. In this unit, you will learn about these processes and the steps used to create their end products. You will also read about some of the skills needed for jobs in the processing industry.

As you read the selections in this unit—everything from a safety poster to a flowchart showing the steps in making yarn—you will gain skills that you will need in all workplaces. Although a lot of the work in processing occupations is done with the hands, thinking and reading skills are important as well.

This unit teaches the following reading skills:

◆ finding the main idea
◆ finding details that support the main idea
◆ understanding visual information

You will learn how workers in the processing industry use these reading skills in their work.

Working in Food Processing

▼▼▼▼▼▼▼▼▼▼▼▼

Words to Know

contaminate

dough

ingredients

manual

manufacturing

production

sanitize

standards

texture

unsanitary

yeast

Processing (PRAHS-ehs-ing) means "using many separate steps to get an end product." Processing canned fruit is different from baking bread. Processing frozen vegetables is different from processing milk. However, all of these processes have some basic principles in common. The food must be fresh. The cooking areas must be clean. The temperature (TEHM-puhr-uh-choor) must be correct. These basic principles are important, no matter which foods are being processed.

It's wise to learn the basics of any job first. Then figuring out the smaller details will be easier. Good workers use this approach when they read, too. As they read, they first try to **find the main idea** in the reading.

The main idea is the most important idea in any reading. The other information relates to the main idea. Often, the main idea is directly stated in a sentence. The main idea also can be stated in a heading or even a title of a selection. Sometimes, however, it is not stated and you have to figure it out from the details. In this lesson, you'll practice finding main ideas in a variety of materials related to food processing.

Job Focus

Bakery workers can perform a wide variety of jobs. It depends on how large or complex the bakery is. Mixer, oven tender, and bench hand are only a few of the jobs available. The work is generally very hard. Bakery workers have to lift and carry heavy bowls of batter from place to place. The work is noisy, and ovens can be very hot.

This industry employs about 40,000 workers, usually in large plants of 100 or more employees. Bakery products must be made year-round since they are usually not frozen. This makes bakery work more stable than some other food processing jobs.

Finding the Main Idea: How It Works

manual (MAN-yoo-ehl)
book of instructions for
employees

The **main idea** is the most important idea in a passage. Read the passage below. It is from a **manual** used by employees at a bakery. As you read, ask yourself, "What is the most important thing that the passage says?"

production (pro-DUK-shun)
the making of something

standards widely
accepted rules

unsanitary
(un-SAN-eh-tair-ee) not
clean

sanitize (SAN-ih-teyez)
make clean

contaminate
(kun-TAM-eh-nayt) to make
unclean and not fit for use

> ## BAKERY MANUAL: SECTION 3
>
> Keeping our food **production** areas clean is an important part of our job. The people who buy our baked goods believe that they are getting food that has been prepared in a clean, safe place. In addition, state health laws require that certain **standards** be met. If our kitchen is found to be **unsanitary**, our plant can be closed. Let's work together to keep our food production areas clean and our baked goods number one in the state.
>
> It is important to **sanitize** all kitchen tools and surfaces. To *sanitize* means to "make clean and germ-free." To do this, you must air-dry this equipment after washing. Using a towel to dry the equipment could **contaminate** it. Put all washed food preparation items on a rack in the drying area. Air-drying will keep your work area clean and germ-free.
>
> *38*   *Sanitary Methods*

Write the main idea of the entire passage.

_____

_____

In the passage above, the main idea is stated, or given, in the first sentence. It says *keeping our food production areas clean is an important part of our job*.

Read the second paragraph. Write the main idea below.

_____

_____

You may have written something like *you must sanitize kitchen equipment by washing and air-drying it*. All of the directions in the paragraph support that idea. It is not directly stated as one sentence, but you can put the ideas together to get that point.

Now read the guidelines below. They are taken from a baker's assistant handbook. As you read, think about the main idea of each section. The main idea may not be directly stated. This main idea could be used as a title or as a heading for the section.

dough (doh) soft, thick mixture of flour and a liquid

ingredients (ihn-GREE-dee-ehnts) things combined together to form a food

yeast (yeest) an ingredient that makes baked goods rise, or puff up

---

TEMPERATURE GUIDELINES

1.1 It is important to maintain the correct **dough** temperature during the baking process. In order to do this, you must keep track of the following three factors:

1. the temperature of the baking area or room
2. the temperature of the dry **ingredients**
3. the temperature of the liquid to be used in the dough.

1.2 Dough without **yeast** needs a temperature of no more than 85°F. Dough with yeast must not go above 95°F. Dough with eggs should not be at a temperature over 120°F.

1.3 Many things can affect the temperature of the dough. Make sure the mixing bowl has not just been washed in hot water. Do not over-mix or under-mix the dough. Over-mixing and under-mixing affect the dough temperature.

1.4 Different kinds of bread need different oven temperatures for baking. Popular American bread is baked at 400 to 425°F. Some French bread is baked at 425 to 475°F. Bread with a lot of sugar, fat, and milk is baked at 350 to 400°F.

1.5 Dough products and their ingredients are stored at different temperatures. Boiled bagels can be kept in a freezer for up to six months. Baked breads, muffins, and cookies can be frozen for up to 90 days. Eggs should never be frozen. Instead, keep them refrigerated at a temperature of 35°F for not more than two weeks.

29   Bakery Methods

Answer the following questions based on the reading selection on page 4.

1. Which of the following titles best describes the main idea of section 1.1?

    a. Use the Same Thermometer (thur-MAHM-ih-tuhr) to Check Temperature

    b. Three Factors Help Maintain Correct Dough Temperature

    c. Check Dough Temperature While Baking

    d. Dry and Liquid Ingredients Affect Temperature

2. Which of the following titles best describes the main idea of section 1.2?

    a. Dough Can Be Mixed Without Yeast

    b. Dough-Making Needs Specific Temperatures

    c. Dough-Making Needs Specific Water Amounts

    d. A Thermometer Is Used for Measuring Dough

3. Which of the following titles best describes the main idea of section 1.3?

    a. A Heated Bowl Can Affect Dough Temperature

    b. Under-Mixing Can Affect Dough Temperature

    c. Many Factors Can Affect Dough Temperature

    d. Over-mixing Can Affect Dough Temperature

4. Which of the following titles best describes the main idea of section 1.4?

    a. All Kinds of Bread Are Baked at the Same Temperature

    b. Oven Temperature Should Never Go Above 425°F

    c. Bread Has a Lot of Sugar, Fat, and Milk

    d. Oven Temperature Depends on What You Are Baking

5. Which of the following titles best describes the main idea of section 1.5?

    a. Not All Foods Should Be Frozen

    b. Eggs Should Never Be Frozen

    c. Freeze Bread for 90 Days

    d. Boiled Bagels Can Be Frozen

Check your answers on page 113.

Anita is a line worker at a large bakery. She went to work for this company three years ago. She held two positions before being promoted to this one.

Anita's first job was to sweep the floors. She worked in the production area. She laughs when she says, "That was the most important job of all. I moved all around the building. I watched what was being done in each area. I learned a lot."

One day, Anita saw a job posting on the employee bulletin board. There was an opening in the sanitation (san-eh-TAY-shun) department. She spoke to her supervisor (SOO-puhr-veyez-ehr), who recommended her for the job. For one year, Anita was part of the sanitation crew. She did daily, weekly, monthly, and yearly cleaning of all the food equipment.

"In the sanitation department, I had to read schedules (SKEHD-joolz) and a handbook," she says. "Each piece of equipment had its own cleaning methods and cleaning schedule. I had to study all the methods in the sanitation handbook. My reading skills got better. Soon I could take the test for my present job."

Anita is a baker's assistant on the dough-mixing line. The biggest part of her job is mixing huge amounts of dough in a giant mixer. She often works with dough that weighs more than she does! Does Anita read on this job? "Of course," she says. "Each order has its own ingredients and needs. The first thing I do is read my work assignments for the day."

TALK ABOUT IT

1. Explain what different kinds of reading Anita does at the bakery.

2. Tell at least three ways reading helped Anita on her job.

If you are deciding what kind of job you would like, it is a good idea to do some research. The library has lots of information about all kinds of workplaces. Read the description below from a pamphlet (PAM-fliht), or booklet, about the food processing industry. Think about the main ideas as you read.

<table>
<tr><td>

manufacturing
(man-yoo-FAK-chur-ihng) the making of things by hand or by machine especially in large amounts

</td><td>

So You Want to Work in Bakery Manufacturing....

▼

A **manufacturing** bakery is an excellent place to work if you like working with food in large amounts. But don't get the idea that you'll be creating new and exciting recipes all day. In a large bakery, different workers perform different parts of the baking process. In general, a supervisor or manager is responsible for choosing recipes. Different teams of workers measure ingredients, combine them, and bake them. So if you're interested in creating your favorite cakes with Aunt Isabel's secret ingredients, use your own kitchen. In a manufacturing bakery, you need to follow strict rules and guidelines at all times.

</td></tr>
<tr><td>

texture (TEKS-chur) the look or feel of something based on its basic materials

</td><td>

A job in baking can be interesting. Each step in the baking process has its own challenges and rewards. For example, *dough mixers* must measure and combine dry and liquid ingredients. They use automatic equipment and often check the temperature and **texture** of the dough. *Dividing machine operators* run the machines that divide and form the dough into loaves, muffins, or cookies. *Bench hands* form dough by using their hands or rolling pins. *Oven tenders* place the dough into huge ovens and remove it when it is finished baking. *Slicing machine operators, decorators,* and *packers,* finish the process.

FOOD PROCESSING INDUSTRY   3

</td></tr>
</table>

Answer the following questions based on the reading selection on page 7.

1. Which of the following sentences states the main idea of the whole passage?

   a. Bakery manufacturing work is difficult but can be interesting.
   b. All jobs in bakery manufacturing are exactly alike.
   c. Following rules and guidelines in bakery manufacturing is very important.
   d. Many workers perform different jobs in bakery manufacturing.

2. Which of the following sentences states the main idea of the first paragraph?

   a. Working at a manufacturing bakery is like working in your own kitchen.
   b. Supervisors usually select the recipes at a manufacturing bakery.
   c. Do not expect to do creative work at a manufacturing bakery.
   d. If you like working indoors, you might think about bakery manufacturing work.

3. Which of the following sentences states the main idea of the second paragraph?

   a. Dough mixing is the first step in a long process.
   b. Each step in the baking process has its own challenges and rewards.
   c. Packing is the last step in the baking process.
   d. Oven tenders place the dough into huge ovens.

4. Which of the following titles best matches the main idea of the whole passage?

   a. Bakery Workers Make Recipes
   b. Bakery Manufacturing Is Tough Work
   c. To Bake It Right, Follow The Rules
   d. Bakery Manufacturing Uses Many Different Workers

Check your answers on page 113.

◆ LESSON WRAP-UP

In this lesson, you learned to find the main idea. The main idea is the most important idea in a reading selection. All of the paragraphs in a passage support the main idea. Likewise, all the sentences in a paragraph support its main idea.

Many times, the main idea of a paragraph will be stated at the beginning, middle, or end. Sometimes, the main idea is used as a title or heading. Other times, you may have to figure it out from the details.

It may help to think of the main idea as a possible title or heading for what you read. The main idea can help you remember what you have read.

When you read a job pamphlet, a page from the employee handbook, a worker's manual, or any other materials, you need to look for the main ideas. Knowing the main ideas will help you understand what you read and apply the information to your job.

1. In what ways do you think understanding main ideas can help you do a job better?

2. What is the difference between a main idea and the other information in a reading selection?

Check your answers on page 113.

Working in Glass Manufacturing

▼▼▼▼▼▼▼▼▼▼▼▼

Words to Know

buffers

cullet

engraved

gauges

grinders

insulated

molten

raw

People have been making glass for thousands of years. Long ago, glass was made by hand, using a method called *glassblowing*. Today, most glass is made in large factories. In this lesson, you'll learn some of the details about working in glass manufacturing.

When you read something on the job, you need to **find the details that support the main idea** as well as find the main ideas. For example, suppose the main idea of a memo is *Many assembly machines have been breaking down*. Supporting details could include examples of which machines broke down, when they broke down, and why. These details "add up" to the most important idea—the main idea.

Why are details important on the job? Often, the main idea is very general. It does not give workers *all* the information they need to do a job well. Details give specific information. They answer such questions as *who? what? when? where? why?* and *how?*

In this lesson, you'll learn about finding details that support the main idea. You'll also learn more about jobs in glass manufacturing.

Job Focus

Glass manufacturing, or production, can be noisy, hot, and smelly. The work can be dangerous, but—with the right equipment—accidents are rare.

It takes a lot of money to heat up a glass-making furnace. So factories often keep the furnaces hot all the time rather than shutting them off at night. Many **glass production workers** staff the night shift—working, for example, from 11:00 P.M. until 7:00 A.M.

The glass industry in the United States now employs about 150,000 workers. More glass workers will be needed as advances are made in many industries that need glass to make their products.

Finding Supporting Details: How It Works

Below is a safety poster that might be found on an employee bulletin board in a glass-making plant. It has a main idea and **supporting details** that explain its main idea. Read the poster. Decide what its main idea is. Then, look for the supporting details.

raw natural; not man-made or processed

> # WORKING WITH GLASS REQUIRES CAUTION!
>
> There are three basic reasons that care must be taken when working with glass:
>
> ☞ <u>Chemicals (KEHM-ih-kuhlz) are used to mix **raw** materials.</u> Breathing in dust, swallowing chemical particles, or handling materials without gloves could result in illness or injury.
>
> ☞ <u>Very high temperatures are used to melt raw materials.</u> Failure to use protective (pruh-TEHKT-ihv) gloves and other clothing will result in serious burns.
>
> ☞ <u>Glass is sharp and can cause cuts if handled carelessly.</u> Even glass in its raw form contains very fine but harmful particles. These particles can damage the skin and eyes.
>
> Keep these facts in mind at all times on the job. Your safety AND that of co-workers depends on it.

The main idea of this poster is that *there are three basic reasons that care must be taken when working with glass.* Think about the details that support this main idea. In other words, which details give more information about the dangers of working with glass?

Notice that a detail that supports the overall main idea can also be the main idea of its own separate paragraph. This main idea can be supported by its own details. For example, *failure to use protective gloves* is a detail that gives more information about the dangers of *using very high temperatures to melt raw materials.*

Use the diagram below to discover how the supporting details support the main idea of the poster. In each box, copy down one sentence that supports the main idea.

DETAIL

| |
| |

+ DETAIL

| |
| |

+ DETAIL

| |
| |

= MAIN IDEA

> **There are three basic reasons that care must be taken when working with glass.**

You might have written these three details: *chemicals are used to mix raw materials, very high temperatures are used to melt raw materials,* and *glass is sharp and can cause cuts if handled carelessly.* If so, you are correct. These details support the main idea of the poster.

Being able to locate and understand details is a very important job skill. A main idea gives you a *general* understanding of something. But a detail provides *specific* information. This information may make the difference between a failure and a job well done.

For example, suppose you read a memo from your company's director. The main idea of the memo is that there are new procedures for closing down workstations. This is the most important idea in the memo. But if you ignore the details, such as when and how closing should take place, you might close down your workstation the wrong way or at the wrong time.

When you read material related to work, first find the main idea. Then ask yourself, "What other information (details) in this passage helps me understand the main idea more clearly?"

Here is a page from a manual for new employees. This page describes the basic process of glass manufacturing. Read it and find the overall main idea. Then, think about the details that support this main idea.

FOUR BASIC STEPS IN MAKING GLASS

Glass can be made into many shapes, forms, and textures. It can be clear or colored. It can be flexible or rigid. It can be soft or hard. No matter what final form glass takes, it becomes glass through this four-step process:

STEP ONE: Raw materials are melted.

cullet (CUL-uht) recycled waste glass

The raw materials include sand, soda ash, limestone, lead oxide (AHKS-yd), and **cullet**. Melting is done in huge furnaces. The furnaces must be kept at very high temperatures for melting to occur.

gauges (GAYJ-uhz) instruments used for measuring or testing

    Gauges must be set properly and adjusted to remove bubbles. The furnace must be well-**insulated** and safe.

insulated (IHN-suh-layt-uhd) covered with material that limits the passage of heat in or out

STEP TWO: The **molten** glass is shaped and formed.

molten (MOHL-tuhn) melted and hot

Molding is most often done by machines. The *blow-molding* method is used to make bottles and containers. The *press-molding* method is used to make flat items such as plates, sheet glass, and trays.

STEP THREE: The formed glass is cooled.

This cooling process is as carefully controlled as the heating process. The glass must not cool too slowly or too quickly.

STEP FOUR: The glass is filed and polished.

grinders (GREYEN-duhrs) materials that shape or refine by using friction

Special **grinders** and **buffers** are used. The glass is decorated or **engraved** if necessary. A final protective coating is sometimes applied.

buffers materials that polish or shine

engraved (ehn-GRAYVD) carved or cut into a hard surface

3

Make an X on the line next to the correct answer to each question. Some questions may have more than one correct answer. Use the employee manual on page 13.

1. What is the overall main idea?

   a._____ Glass is shaped and formed.
   b._____ There are four basic steps in making glass.
   c._____ Glass can be clear, colored, flexible, or rigid.
   d._____ In Step One, raw materials are melted.

2. What is the main idea of Step One?

   a._____ Raw materials are melted.
   b._____ Molten glass is shaped and formed.
   c._____ The formed glass is cooled.
   d._____ The glass is filed and polished.

3. Which details support the main idea of Step One?

   a._____ Basic raw materials include sand, soda ash, limestone, lead oxide, and cullet.
   b._____ Melting is done in huge furnaces.
   c._____ The temperature must be very high.
   d._____ A final protective coating is applied.

4. Which details support the main idea of Step Two?

   a._____ Molding is most often done by machines.
   b._____ The *blow-molding* method is used to make bottles and containers.
   c._____ The *press-molding* method is used to make flat items such as plates, sheet glass, and trays.
   d._____ The formed glass is cooled.

5. Which details support the main idea of Step Three?

   a._____ The cooling process must be carefully controlled.
   b._____ Raw materials are melted.
   c._____ The cooling process is controlled as much as the heating process.
   d._____ The glass must not cool too slowly or too quickly.

6. Which details support the main idea of Step Four?

a._____ Glass can be clear or colored.

b._____ Special grinders and buffers are used.

c._____ The glass is decorated or engraved if necessary.

d._____ A final protective coating is sometimes applied.

Check your answers on page 113.

ON THE JOB

Paul Wong has been a furnace tender in the glass manufacturing industry for over five years. He was asked to speak at a new employee meeting. He told the newly hired workers what he thought was most important in his job.

"Teamwork and attention to details are important," he said. "If you keep those two things in mind, you'll do well here."

Later, Paul explained what he meant by teamwork. "For example," he said, "I'm the one who makes sure that air, fuel, and water pressure inside the furnace are just right. I work with other team members to complete this step. It's harder for me if other team members don't read the work order right and add 10 percent cullet instead of 20 percent. There's no way I can come up with the proper molten glass for that order. I count on my team members to send me the right stuff. Likewise, the people down in molding and shaping count on me to deliver quality."

Paul also explained why details are important on the job. On my job every day, I read work orders that tell me what my settings need to be on all my gauges. I may have to start a job at 2700 degrees and then change it a bit to remove bubbles. Reading the details of the work order helps me make good decisions and stay on top of the job."

TALK ABOUT IT

1. Discuss why reading details is an important skill on Paul's job.

2. When in your own life have teamwork and attention to details been important? Explain.

No matter how careful workers are, there is always the possibility of an accident on the job. Knowing how to handle an emergency is very important. Posted at Paul's workstation are steps to follow in case of a burn. Read the notice below. Use details to answer the questions that follow it.

EMERGENCY!
In case of burn . . .

Follow these simple steps to help someone with a burn:

▶ Pull the EMERGENCY CALL cord at your workstation.

▶ Immediately apply the ice pack to the burned skin. An emergency ice pack is in the first aid kit in the storage chest.

▶ DO NOT apply any cream or lotion at this time.

▶ Further treatment differs depending on the degree of the burn. See the company nurse IMMEDIATELY to find out if antibiotics (an-ty-by-AHT-ihks) are needed to kill any germs.

▶ Report all accidents to the safety and protection supervisor. Fill out an accident report if asked.

CHECK YOUR UNDERSTANDING

Circle **TRUE** or **FALSE** for each statement below.

TRUE FALSE **1.** An employee should dial 911 if he or she is burned.

TRUE FALSE **2.** The emergency ice pack can be found at the nurse's station.

TRUE FALSE **3.** An ice pack should be applied immediately to the affected area.

TRUE FALSE **4.** An antibiotic is always the best treatment for a burn.

TRUE FALSE **5.** An emergency call cord is located in the plant manager's office.

TRUE FALSE **6.** If you follow the steps given, you will not get burned.

TRUE FALSE **7.** Cream or lotion should not be applied to a burn right away.

Check your answers on page 113.

◆ LESSON WRAP-UP

You have now learned how to find supporting details. You looked at some reading selections. You have learned how details support the main idea, which is the most important idea in a passage.

DETAIL
+ DETAIL
+ DETAIL
+ DETAIL
= MAIN IDEA

Details support the main idea by giving more specific information about it. Details can answer the questions *who? what? when? where? why?* and *how?*

When you read something on the job, first try to find the main idea. But don't stop there! You found out from Paul Wong's speech that the details in a reading selection are very important. On a job, details can make the difference between success and failure—or safety and injury.

1. What details did you learn about making glass in this lesson? List as many as you would like.

   DETAIL:

   DETAIL:

   DETAIL:

   DETAIL:

2. What main idea do these details support?

   MAIN IDEA:

Check your answers on page 113.

Working in Textile Manufacturing

Words to Know

bales

fibers

roving

sliver

spools

starch

yarn

Textile (TEHK-steyel) manufacturing is another processing industry. In this lesson, you'll learn about the textile-manufacturing process, or how cloth is made.

Processes are described in many ways. Perhaps you have read passages with labels such as "Step One," "Step Two," "Step Three," and so on. Or perhaps you have seen numbers used to list the steps in a step-by-step process.

Sometimes, information you read on the job is not written in step-by-step form. Instead, it may be in the form of drawings and words. Studying this visual information can be an easy way to understand a process. You do less reading, and information is easy to find.

Understanding visual information is an important skill to have on the job. One kind of visual found on the job is a flowchart (FLOH-chahrt). Such a chart uses boxes containing words and connecting arrows to describe a process. In this lesson, you'll learn how to read a flowchart. You'll also learn about the process of making cloth, or textile manufacturing.

Job Focus

Work in a modern textile plant is usually efficient and comfortable. Most **textile workers** operate different machines that perform steps in the manufacturing process. Jobs can involve doing the same task over and over, but textile workers need to be alert at all times. Although machines do a lot of the work, only human beings can assure the quality of a product. The work is not hard, but most textile workers have to stand up most of the day.

The more automated the textile process becomes, the more skilled a worker needs to be. Today, there are about 650,000 workers in textile mills across the country.

Understanding Visual Information: How It Works

Workers who need to learn the steps of a process need to **understand visual information.** For example, processes are often explained in a flowchart.

Below are two examples describing the cloth-making process. The first example is in paragraph form. The second example is a flowchart. Each step in the flowchart appears in its own box. An arrow directs you to the next step. Read both examples.

yarn raw or man-made fibers twisted into strands

bales (baylz) large, bound bundles of raw or finished materials

fibers (FEYE-buhrs) threadlike strands of cotton, wool, or nylon

sliver (SLY-vuhr) a long, loose rope of fibers

roving (ROHV-ihng) several slivers twisted together

The Cloth-Making Process
YARN MANUFACTURING

There are three major stages in making cloth in a factory. The first stage is *yarn manufacturing.* The second stage is *fabric construction.* The last stage is called *finishing.* Each of these stages, however, has several steps. Let's take a closer look at the first stage.

In the yarn manufacturing stage, huge **bales** of raw **fibers** are fed into machines. Next, carding machines straighten the fibers and coil them into a long, loose rope, called a **sliver.** Then several slivers are pulled together into a single strand, called a **roving.** Next, a spinning frame operator threads the roving through a frame that combines six or eight rovings to make the yarn. Finally, the yarn is examined to be sure it has nothing wrong with it.

Yarn Manufacturing Flowchart

| Opened bales of fiber are fed into machines. |

↓

| The carding machine untangles and coils fibers into slivers. |

↓

| Several slivers form a roving, or single strand. |

↓

| The roving is twisted into yarn on a spinning frame. |

↓

| **THE YARN IS EXAMINED.** |

What is the second step of the yarn manufacturing process?

_____

_____

You're correct if you said *the carding machine untangles and coils fibers into slivers.* What happens after the yarn is examined? Why do you think the words are written in capital letters?

_____

_____

_____

On many flowcharts, different parts of a process are pointed out by the use of capital and small letters, shapes, and even colors. You were correct if you said that *after the yarn is examined, the next stage, fabric construction, begins.* You might have added, *then, the fabric goes through the finishing stage.*

Here is a flowchart that describes the steps in the fabric construction process—how fabric is made from yarn. Look at the flowchart carefully.

Fabric Construction Flowchart

spools rods with a rim at each end and a hole through the middle

starch a substance that stiffens fabrics and yarns

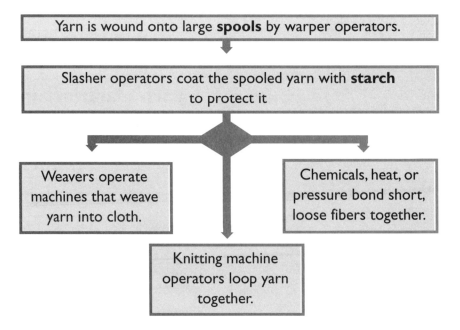

Yarn is wound onto large **spools** by warper operators.

Slasher operators coat the spooled yarn with **starch** to protect it

Weavers operate machines that weave yarn into cloth.

Chemicals, heat, or pressure bond short, loose fibers together.

Knitting machine operators loop yarn together.

LESSON 3 ◆ WORKING IN TEXTILE MANUFACTURING

Answer the following questions using the flowchart on page 20.

1. How many steps are there in the fabric construction process?

2. What is the first step of the fabric construction process?

3. What three steps can complete the fabric construction process?

1.

2.

3.

4. What is the role of the slasher operator?

5. What are three ways in which short, loose fibers can be bonded together?

Check your answers on page 113.

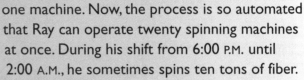

Ray Ivers has been operating spinning machines at Clover Textile Company for six years. When he started, he operated one machine. Now, the process is so automated that Ray can operate twenty spinning machines at once. During his shift from 6:00 P.M. until 2:00 A.M., he sometimes spins ten tons of fiber.

For several hours at a time, he walks up and down the row of spinning machines. He makes sure that there is a good supply of sliver entering the machines. He replaces empty spools of sliver with full ones.

However, Ray's job is not always just tending the machines. He also is responsible for reading the process orders each day. "Each order has its own process," he tells a visitor. "The yarn for each order has to be made a specific weight. It has to be set up on the right spinner. I have to read the order and set the controls correctly. All instructions are included on the work flowchart."

The part of Ray's job that he likes best is quality control. He must always watch out for breaks or pulls in the yarn. He must stop the machine right away if the yarn is not good quality. He must also limit the number of shutdowns to as few as possible. Otherwise, he will get behind in his orders. "It's sometimes hard to decide whether I should shut down a spinner. I take pride in the quality of my yarn. I want it to be perfect."

TALK ABOUT IT

1. List the kinds of reading that Ray Ivers does on the job.

2. What might happen if Ray does not read carefully?

Read these two examples of textile plant work orders. You will answer questions about the work orders below. Then you will make a flowchart.

Textile Work Orders

Batch #451A

B Shift:	B Shift:	C Shift:	A Shift:	B Shift:
open & clean	blend	card	comb & draw	spin
date: 5/8	date: 5/8	date: 5/9	date: 5/10	date: 5/11

Batch #ER216

A Shift:	B Shift:	C Shift:	C Shift:	D Shift:
open & clean	blend	card	comb & draw	spin
date: 6/1	date: 6/1	date: 6/2	date: 6/3	date: 6/3

CHECK YOUR UNDERSTANDING

Use the work orders above to answer questions 1–4.

1. Which step does the C shift perform for batch #451A?

2. On what day(s) does the B shift work on batch #451A?

3. For batch #ER216, which step follows the blending step?

4. Which of the two batches goes through the whole process more quickly?

5. Read the description of the finishing process on page 24. Use the information to create your own flowchart.

The Cloth-Making Process
FINISHING

To *finish a piece of cloth* means "to put it through treatments that will give it a special look." Finishes can make cloth repel water, resist flame, or hold its color. Depending on the desired look, a textile batch can go through anywhere from one to more than 500 finishing techniques. Here's an example:

First, Batch 1 of cotton is boiled to remove the natural gums found in the raw materials. Next, it is bleached to make it pure white in color. Starch is then applied to strengthen the cotton for weaving into cloth. The shrinkage-control process is applied to the cloth. Following this, the cloth is "puffed up" to reduce differences between various cottons used in the cloth.

Finish the following flowchart with five boxes. The first has been done for you.

Finishing Flow Chart

Boil

↓

Check your answers on page 113.

◆ LESSON WRAP-UP

Not all reading material is written in paragraph form. Processes are often explained in a visual form. Understanding this visual information is an important reading skill on the job.

A flowchart is an example of visual information. A flowchart breaks a process down into steps. It uses a series of shapes, words, and arrows to show what comes next. Note the steps in this flowchart for finishing cloth by dyeing.

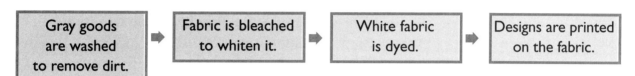

1. Draw a flowchart describing how you spend an average day. Use shapes, words, and arrows to show the steps in your day.

Average-Day Flow Chart

2. Now draw a flowchart showing how you would *like* to spend your day. Be creative!

Perfect-Day Flow Chart

Check your answers on page 114.

◆ UNIT ONE REVIEW

1. Write a paragraph that describes the difference between a main idea and a supporting detail. Be sure to include definitions in your paragraph.

2. Give three examples that tell why understanding details is important in the workplace. You can make up examples, or give some from real life.

    a.

    b.

    c.

3. Write a paragraph that describes what a flowchart is. Tell why it is used and what the advantages are.

4. Of the jobs described in this unit—bakery worker, glass furnace tender, and spinning frame operator— which one appeals to you most? Why?

Check your answers on page 114.

Machine Trades
• Occupations •

The jobs you will focus on in Unit Two are **machine trades occupations.** As machines perform more and more tasks, people are needed to operate, maintain, and repair these machines. People who work in the machine trades might service automobiles, fix broken vending machines, operate machine tools, or do hundreds of other tasks related to machines. In this unit, you will learn more about these types of jobs and the skills needed to perform them.

As you read the selections in this unit—everything from a troubleshooting guide to a time card—you will gain reading and thinking skills that are useful in all workplaces. Jobs in the machine trades require workers to be able to read a variety of materials. Then they must show their understanding of the material by applying it directly to their work.

This unit teaches the following reading skills:

◆ identifying cause and effect
◆ comparing and contrasting
◆ understanding visual information

You will learn how workers in the machine trades use these reading skills in their work.

Servicing Automobiles

One of the most satisfying jobs in the skilled trades is automobile repair. Many automobile mechanics (mih-KAN-ihks) feel pride when they can get a vehicle (VEE-ih-kuhl) running again. Why? Most people depend on cars to get them to work, home, and the store.

An important step in automobile service is figuring out what is wrong with a car. When something is wrong, the owner may not know what the problem is. All the owner knows is that the car isn't working right. Perhaps it is making strange noises. Maybe the headlights won't go on. In other words, the owner knows the **effect** of a problem, but not the **cause.**

The auto mechanic's job is to find out the cause of the problem and to fix it. Is the battery dead? Has an electrical (ih-LEHK-trih-kuhl) fuse been blown? Is there a muffler problem?

Identifying cause and effect is an important skill on the job. It is also an important reading skill. When reading work-related material, an employee needs to be able to figure out whether something is a cause or an effect.

Job Focus

Automobile mechanics, also called auto technicians (tehk-NIHSH-uhnz), use a variety of machines and tools, as well as their hands. Auto mechanics can specialize in certain systems, such as transmissions (trans-MIHSH-uhnz), brakes, or exhaust (ihg-ZAWST) systems. Or a mechanic can do repairs. The work is often dirty, since mechanics use grease and oil. Automobile mechanics have to figure out problems, so they are usually patient, logical thinkers.

Today, more than 700,000 people are employed as auto mechanics. The outlook for skilled auto mechanics is good.

Identifying Cause and Effect: How It Works

It is important to know how to **identify cause and effect.** A cause is what makes something happen. An effect is what happens. Many ideas and events are connected in cause-and-effect relationships.

Read the typical work order below. It is for employee Dan Farson. He is an auto mechanic at Arnie's Car Repair. As you read, pay attention to any causes or effects.

Arnie's Car Repair — **Work Order**

Mechanic: _DF_

Date: _Monday, July 2_

Vehicle description: _1995 Chevrolet_

Customer complaints:

1) _The car starts fine, but engine does not run smoothly._

2) _There is more smoke than usual when driving._

Possible problems:

- ☑ dirty fuel filter
- ☐ loose muffler
- ☐ worn brake pads
- ☑ faulty air filter
- ☑ loose or damaged vacuum (VAHK-yoom) hose
- ☐ radiator (RAY-dee-ayt-er) leak

Two effects were reported by the customer. If you thought that an *engine not running smoothly* and *too much smoke* were the effects, you were right. What were the possible causes that Dan wanted to look for? The check marks next to the items told you that he suspected a *dirty fuel filter,* a *faulty air filter,* and a *loose or damaged vacuum hose.* Dan checked each one and found that a damaged vacuum hose was the cause of the problem.

Here's a diagram of this cause-and-effect relationship:

CAUSES		EFFECTS
damaged vacuum hose		engine not running smoothly too much smoke

Words and phrases such as *because, as a result, due to, therefore, if,* and *so* often signal a cause-and-effect relationship. Look for these words and phrases as you read.

Read each sentence below. Draw one line under each cause and two lines under each effect.

For example:
Renee's car would not start because it was out of gas.

1. Jorge's car battery was dead, so he called the emergency road service.
2. The gas station attendant spilled oil on Theo's engine. As a result, smoke poured out from under the car's hood.
3. Due to ice in the **carburetor**, Ms. Tomas's car was running poorly.
4. Jim Chun could not keep track of the distance he traveled because the **odometer** was broken.

Use the sentences and your underlines to fill in the cause-and-effect chart below. The first one is done for you.

carburetor
(KAHR-buh-ray-tuhr) a device for mixing air with fuel in a car's engine

odometer
(oh-DAHM-ih-tuhr) an instrument (IHN-struh-muhnt) on the dashboard of a vehicle that measures distance traveled

CAUSES		EFFECTS
The car was out of gas.		Renee's car would not start.
_____		_____
_____		_____
_____		_____

CAUSES	EFFECTS
The car was out of gas.	Renee's car would not start.
Jorge's car battery was dead.	Jorge called for road service.
Oil was spilled on Theo's engine.	Smoke poured out from under the hood.
There was ice in the carburetor.	Ms. Tomas's car was running poorly.
The odometer was broken.	Jim Chun couldn't keep track of the distance he traveled.

Mechanics can use a troubleshooting guide to help them solve problems. For example, Dan can use the troubleshooting guide in his automotive handbook. It will help him figure out what is wrong with a car brought in for repairs. Read this page from his guide, and then answer the questions.

vibrates (VEYE-brayts) moves back and forth rapidly

alignment (uh-LEYEN-muhnt) arrangement in a straight line

tire pressure (PREHSH-uhr) amount of compressed air inside a tire

lug nuts caps that fit over a bolt

shock absorber (uhb-ZAWRB-uhr) car part that takes up the impact of bumps on the road

steering linkage (STEER-ihng LIHNG-kihj) connection between the steering wheel and the tires

BASIC WHEEL/ TIRE PROBLEMS

Problem	Possible Cause
• front end **vibrates** when car travels at high speed	• wheels out of **alignment** • wheels unbalanced
• car pulls to right or left	• wheels out of alignment • unequal **tire pressure**
• car wheel(s) wobble or shake	• loose wheel **lug nuts** • damaged wheel • defective **shock absorber** • worn parts in **steering linkage**
• tires wear unevenly or too soon	• incorrect wheel size • wheels unbalanced

Use the troubleshooting guide on page 31 and your understanding of cause and effect to answer the questions.

1. A customer brings his car into your repair shop and tells you that the wheels shake when he drives. What are *two* possible causes for this problem?

    a. loose lug nuts
    b. unbalanced wheels
    c. unequal tire pressure
    d. damaged wheel

2. After inspecting a customer's car, you find the tire pressure is unequal. What might the effect of this be?

    a. front end vibration
    b. wobbling or shaking car wheels
    c. gas leakage
    d. car pulling to right or left

3. A customer calls and says her front tires are very worn, but her back tires look brand new. What are *two* possible causes for this effect?

    a. wheels out of alignment
    b. incorrect wheel size
    c. unbalanced wheels
    d. loose lug nuts

Write two sentences that link a cause to an effect. Use the troubleshooting guide on page 31. Use any of the following connecting words: *because, as a result, due to, so.*

For example: *Because the wheels are out of alignment, the front end vibrates.*

4.

5.

Check your answers on page 115.

Jane Carter grew up around cars. Both her parents fixed old automobiles as a hobby, so Jane knew the working parts of a car at a very young age. She has always enjoyed watching people take machines apart, fix them, and put them back together. It is no surprise that she has become an auto mechanic.

Jane learns most things on her job by doing. Her supervisor shows her how to install gas struts, for example. Then she performs the same steps on another car. Her supervisor watches her and makes some suggestions and corrections. Then she tries again. When she has a question, she asks another mechanic or her supervisor for help.

Sometimes, however, a customer may come in with a car problem that is unfamiliar to Jane and the other mechanics. Or she may be the only mechanic working at the time. This is when Jane's reading skills are important. Fortunately, the repair shop shelves are filled with manuals for many different cars. She uses these materials to look up a problem (effect) and to find out what the reason for the problem (cause) might be. Because there are so many models of cars, it is impossible to know everything about every make and model. That's why Jane's reading skills are important on the job.

TALK ABOUT IT

1. Jane learns skills mostly by doing them as her supervisor watches. Explain why she also needs good reading skills.

2. Discuss other kinds of reading Jane might be required to do as an auto mechanic.

Here is part of a page from a service manual for a minivan. It describes the servicing procedures for the air conditioning system. This type of material is required reading for new mechanics in many auto repair shops. Read the manual and answer the questions that follow it.

refrigerant
(rih-FRIHJ-uhr-uhnt) liquid used for cooling

V.2 AIR CONDITIONING SYSTEMS

The most important part of air conditioning service is checking the **refrigerant**. You must keep the refrigerant clean and charged. An air conditioning system cannot work correctly if the charge is lost.

Watch out for leaks. Leaks are common because automobiles vibrate and the air conditioning fittings can crack or loosen. If this happens, refrigerant flows out.

Skin contact with refrigerant will cause frostbite. Wear protective gloves and clothing when working with refrigerant.

Use only refrigerant #12. Do not use refrigerant that is made for other purposes, such as for cleaning a horn. This type of refrigerant is not pure. It will cause failure in your air conditioning system.

CHECK YOUR UNDERSTANDING

Answer the questions below with either a cause or an effect. Base your answers on the passage above.

1. A mechanic forgot to put on gloves when he poured refrigerant. Some splashed on his left hand. As a result,

2. The refrigerant used at Bob's Station was not kept clean and charged. So, when Justin had his car serviced this summer,

3. A customer reported that refrigerant was leaking from her car. What may have been the cause?

4. The mechanic added refrigerant from an unlabeled can to the air conditioning system in Kim's station wagon. The system may have failed because

Check your answers on page 115.

◆ LESSON WRAP-UP

Identifying cause and effect is an important reading skill on the job. If you understand what is a cause and what is an effect, you will be better able to find a solution.

When you read, be on the lookout for signal words such as: *because, so, as a result, therefore, if,* and *due to.* These words are clues that a cause-and-effect connection is being made in a passage. Sometimes, it is good practice to actually underline the cause and the effect in a sentence containing one of these signal words.

Add a cause or an effect to each sentence started below. Then, draw one line under each cause and two lines under each effect.

1. I want to get and keep a well-paying job. Therefore,

2. If a person
he or she will have lots of good friends.

3. Because reading skills are important on the job, I

4. Write three more sentences describing a cause-and-effect relationship from your own life.

Check your answers on page 115.

Working With Machines

Words to Know

blueprints

boring

conveyor belt

drill press

grinder

lathe

malfunctioning

precision

rotating

Suppose you are interested in working with machines. You like taking things apart and putting them back together. All machine work has some things in common. But there are also some important differences. You can work as a machine tool operator. That means you work on one type of machine. Or you can work as a general, all-around machinist (muh-SHEEN-ihst). You can work in a large factory, or you can work in a small machine shop.

Comparing and contrasting will help you make a decision about the type of machine work you might like to do. *Comparing* is "finding ways things are alike." *Contrasting* is "finding ways things are different." In this lesson, you'll compare and contrast two machine-work jobs while learning this important reading skill.

Before you begin, think about the work that machinists might do. What kinds of machine tools might they operate? What kinds of materials would they make with their machine tools?

Job Focus

In this lesson, you'll learn about the jobs of **machine tool operator** and general, all-around **machinist**. A machine tool operator works only on one type of machine that shapes metal by cutting, drilling, filing, hammering, or squeezing. A machinist is someone who has a general, all-around knowledge of how to machine metals such as steel, brass, or copper into usable parts. The work can be repetitive, but workers must stay alert at all times. A machine shop is often noisy and dirty. The work is most often indoors, year-round.

The number of jobs for machine industry workers is expected to stay about the same through the year 2000.

Comparing and Contrasting: How It Works

The following page is taken from a machine company training manual. Read the two jobs. In what ways are the jobs alike, and in what ways are they different?

Machine Shop Training Manual   64

JACK is a machinist at a small machine shop called Top Machines, Inc. He is the only machinist employed there, and he operates all four of the machines. Part of his day is spent reading **blueprints** and planning which tools and materials he'll need. He also spends time servicing or cleaning the machines so that they run well. However, he spends most of his day operating the machines. The ones he works with are an automatic **lathe**, a **drill press**, a **grinder**, and a screw machine. Jack is on his feet all day.

VERONICA works at a large machine factory. She is a machine tool operator, and she stands most of the day at a turning and **boring** machine. Her job is to put metal parts into a holder, and to operate the machine so that the holes bored into each part are exact, or correct. The machine is preset to cut with **precision** at a very high rate of speed. At certain times, Veronica checks the quality of a finished part to make sure its measurements are exact. For most of the workday, Veronica performs these tasks over and over.

---

blueprints (BLOO-prihnts) carefully designed plans or technical drawings

lathe (layth) machine tool for cutting and shaping metals

drill press machine tool for making holes in metal

grinder (GREYEN-dehr) machine tool for finishing or sharpening metal pieces

boring (BOHR-ihng) making a hole in or through a piece of metal by machine tool

precision (prih-SIHZH-uhn) exactness; very little error

Below is a diagram with two overlapping circles. The diagram compares and contrasts Jack's and Veronica's jobs. The items listed in the center section where the circles overlap are the ways the jobs are alike. The items listed outside the center section describe the ways the jobs are different.

Jack, all-around machinist   **Veronica, machine tool operator**

works at small shop
operates four machines
spends time reading and planning
services and cleans the machines

operates machinery
spends day standing

works at large factory
operates one machine
performs same task most of the workday
checks measurements

The two jobs compared and contrasted on page 37 were described in two separate paragraphs. Many things you read, both on the job and in everyday life, compare and contrast two things in the same piece of writing. When things are being compared and contrasted, expect to find "clue words." Some contrast clue words are: *but, however, while,* and *on the other hand.* Some compare clue words are: *both, same, in common,* and *similar.*

Read the paragraph below. The paragraph compares and contrasts the day shift and the night shift. As you read, underline any clue words. Then complete the diagram in the same way as in the example on page 37.

On both the day shift and the night shift, you still have to work eight hours. But working the day shift has one big advantage. You are working when most people work. On the other hand, working the night shift means that you have your day free to do daytime errands. Seeing family and friends is usually easier when nights are free. But free days can mean less need for child care. You might have a family to take care of your children at night. However, no matter which shift you work, you have to get used to the schedule.

What clue words did you underline?

_____

You should have underlined *both, but, on the other hand,* and *however.*

Label the circles below. Then fill in the ways the shifts are alike and the ways they are different.

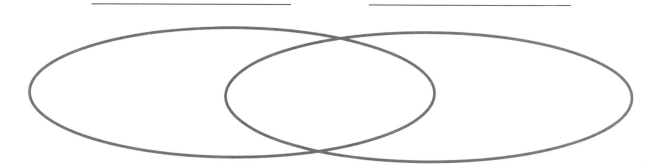

Did you find that the ways the shifts are alike are *you have to work eight hours* and *you have to get used to the schedule?* If so, you are correct.

Did you also find the following differences?

Day shift	Night shift
work when most people work	can do errands in daytime
can see family and friends at night	less need for child care

There are two methods of shutting down the KX-110 turning machine. The reading selection below describes the two methods as well as how and why it is shut down. Read the selection and answer the questions that follow it.

2.6

KX-110 SHUTDOWN

■■■■■■■■■■■■■■■■■■■■■■■■■■

Both the SHUT DOWN position on the power dial and the EMERGENCY STOP pushbutton on the panel turn off the KX-110. The SHUT DOWN position on the dial stops the **conveyor belt** and the **rotating** arm, while EMERGENCY STOP pushbutton cuts off all electrical power. Use SHUT DOWN to stop work for a short time. However, use EMERGENCY STOP in the case of fire, injury, or serious **malfunctioning** of the machine. After using SHUT DOWN, restart simply by turning the dial to AUTO START. On the other hand, to restart after an EMERGENCY STOP, you must begin at step 3.1 outlined on page 47 of this manual. Both methods of turning off the KX-110 do not affect materials in the machine.

■■■■■■■■■■■■■■■■■■■■■■■■■■

Section 2   35

conveyor (kuhn-VAY-uhr) **belt** moving belt that moves things from one place to another

rotating (ROH-tayt-ihng) turning or spinning

malfunctioning (mal-FUHNGK-shuhn-ihng) not working correctly

Answer the following questions based on the reading selection on page 39.

1. What two things are being compared and contrasted?

2. What two ways are they alike?

3. Name three differences.

4. Which of the following are compare/contrast clue words from this selection? Circle all that apply.

position	after	or
however	all	step
both	while	on the other hand

5. Suppose a worker correctly pressed the EMERGENCY STOP button. Which of the following could be the reason or reasons for this action? More than one answer may be correct.

    a. to stop the conveyor belt
    b. to stop work for a short time
    c. to stop because of fire
    d. to stop because of injury
    e. to make sure that no materials would be affected

6. Where can a machinist turn in the manual for information about how to restart the machine after an emergency stop?

Check your answers on page 115.

Ted is a machinist for a large plant that makes thousands of high-quality metal parts every day. The parts are shipped to factories, where they are used for making telephones and stereo equipment.

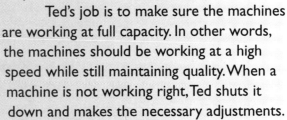

Ted's job is to make sure the machines are working at full capacity. In other words, the machines should be working at a high speed while still maintaining quality. When a machine is not working right, Ted shuts it down and makes the necessary adjustments.

Ted came to this job through a program made available by his union—the International Association of Machinists. He spent close to 600 hours in a classroom and more than 6,000 hours training as an apprentice (uh-PREHN-tihs). As an apprentice, Ted worked with a skilled worker who taught him the basics of machinery as well as filing, drilling, and lathe work. In the classroom and with the skilled worker, Ted learned how to read blueprints.

What kind of reading does Ted do on the job regularly? He says that the most important thing he reads is the information on the employee bulletin board. "As employees, we are required to stay informed about what is going on at the plant. Most of the time, the only way to do this is to read the notices on the board. That's where we get our weekly schedule, any new job postings, all safety and inspection information, and news of upcoming orders."

TALK ABOUT IT

1. Discuss the types of reading that Ted does on the job.

2. What might be the advantages of working as an apprentice? Explain.

Comparing and contrasting is a good way to make a job decision. It is a good idea to compare the features, benefits, and working conditions of several jobs. The selection below, describing two worksites, is taken from an employment opportunity guide. Read the selection, and then answer the questions.

HIGHSITE MANUFACTURING COMPANY

Highsite is a large plant, employing over 500 workers. The main plant operates around the clock. Most workers work the same machine tool all the time and are on their feet most of the day. Some workers specialize in service and repair of machines. Entry-level machinists earn $478 per week. Opportunities for promotion are excellent.

MAC'S MACHINE SHOP

A machinist at Mac's works on a variety of small machines each day. Because there are only five machinists on duty, each one is responsible for everything from operating machines to cleaning and oiling them to general cleanup. Some of the work can be done outdoors, sitting at a temporary workbench. Machinists at this small shop earn $420 per week. Machinists report to one shop foreman.

CHECK YOUR UNDERSTANDING

Complete the following compare/contrast sentences.

1. Highsite Manufacturing is a large plant, whereas Mac's Machine Shop

2. Machinists at Mac's work on a variety of machines; on the other hand, at Highsite,

3. Workers stand all day at Highsite, while at Mac's

4. Write a sentence that compares wages at Highsite Manufacturing and Mac's Machine Shop.

Check your answers on page 115.

In this lesson, you learned about comparing and contrasting. You practiced deciding what is similar and what is different about certain machinist jobs. As you discovered, you can learn and make decisions better when you compare and contrast two things.

You learned to look for clue words that show contrast. Some of these words include: *however, but, on the other hand,* and *while.* You also learned words that compare, such as *both* and *same.*

As you read on the job, be aware that comparing and contrasting help you think clearly. Finish this sentence:

1. When two things are being compared and contrasted, the writer is describing

Now, think of two things you would like to compare and contrast. They could be two jobs, two foods, or even two people.

2. Make a circle diagram below to compare and contrast these two things.

3. Use the information in the diagram to write a paragraph about what you are comparing and contrasting. Use clue words such as those given in the second paragraph above.

Check your answers on page 116.

Servicing Vending Machines

At one time or another, you probably have put coins into a machine and pressed a button to buy something. Such a machine is called a *vending machine*. In this lesson, you'll learn about the job of servicing vending machines. You'll also find out about some of the reading that is done by vending machine service workers. Some of the information they need to do their job is given in easy-to-read visuals.

Most of the reading we do in the workplace is in paragraph form—just like the reading you are doing now. In paragraph form, several sentences based on a main idea are written together.

Information is not always given in paragraph form. In some jobs, workers use information in visual form. These workers need to **understand visual information.**

One way to give visual information is a **table.** Usually, complete sentences are not used in a table. Instead, words and numbers are in columns and rows. This format makes specific information easy to find. Reading a table can often be faster than reading whole paragraphs.

Job Focus

A trained **vending machine service worker** installs, maintains, and repairs machines that sell small items and services. About 20,000 vending machine service workers are employed in the United States. Vending machine service workers go from place to place and deal directly with their customers. This can be a satisfying job for someone who doesn't like to stay in one place all day.

Understanding Visual Information: How It Works

You need two steps to **understand visual information** in a table. First, you read the title to find out what information is given. Then, you read across the rows and down the columns to find the information you need.

The time card below is a sample of a table that many employees see and use on the job. This time card is used by Nick Freewald.

TIME CARD: Hours Worked in MARCH						
Name: Nick Freewald Social Security #: 000-00-1000				Employee #: 3212 Supervisor: B. Fortin		
Week	Monday	Tuesday	Wednesday	Thursday	Friday	Sat./Sun.
3/1–3/7	8	5	8	5	10	10
3/8–3/14	8	8	sick day	8	8	8
3/15–3/21	10	7	8	8	10	10
3/22–3/28	all day meeting	8	8	6	company picnic	0
3/29–3/31	8	8	8			

What information is given in the title of the time card?

_____

_____

You are right if you said that *the time card tells the number of hours worked in March.*

Suppose you wanted to know how many hours Nick Freewald worked on Tuesday during the week of March 15. Read across the rows and down the columns to find out. Follow these steps:

	COLUMN	COLUMN
ROW		
ROW		
ROW		

1. Find the column labeled *Tuesday*. Columns run up and down.
2. Find the row labeled *3/15-3/21*. Rows run left to right.
3. Read across this row and down this column to find the point where they meet, or intersect.

How many hours did he work that day?_____
You are correct if you said *8*.

In what week and on what day did Nick take a sick day?

_____

How many hours did Nick work on the weekend during
the week of 3/22 _____

On how many days between 3/1 and 3/28 did Nick put
in over 8 hours? _____

You have a good grasp of reading tables if you answered:
Wednesday during the week of March 8; 0; and *5.*

The table below shows a maintenance (MAYNT-nehns)
schedule used by a vending machine company. Read
it, and then answer the questions that follow.

Maintenance Schedule: Beverage Plus, Inc.				
	DAILY	WEEKLY	MONTHLY	YEARLY
Remove all money and record total.	✓			
Refill empty liquid **canisters.**	✓			
Run two practice tests.		✓		
Check temperature gauges.		✓		
Check and clean electrical and water connections.		✓		
Recalibrate dispenser.			✓	
Use **lubricant** on all moving parts and **chute.**			✓	
Take machine for tune-up.				✓

canisters (KAN-ih-stuhrz)
large containers for holding
liquids

recalibrate
(ree-KAL-uh-brayt) fix,
check, or correct
measurements again

lubricant (LOO-brih-kuhnt)
slippery substance, such as
oil, used to coat the surfaces
of working parts

chute (shoot) slanting
passage, down which things
are dropped

CHECK YOUR UNDERSTANDING

For each question, circle the correct answers based on the schedule
above. Some questions may have more than one correct answer.

1. Temperature gauges should be checked

    a. daily   b. weekly   c. monthly

2. Vending machine money should be removed and counted

   a. daily   b. weekly   c. monthly

3. Tasks that should be performed monthly are:

   a. Recalibrate dispenser.
   b. Use lubricant on all moving parts and chute.
   c. Bring machine in for tune-up.

4. How often should the two practice tests be run?

   a. weekly   b. monthly   c. yearly

Check your answers on page 116.

ON THE JOB

Pamela Canton works as a vending machine service worker. At the office, Pamela goes over her schedule with her supervisor and maps out the best route. Today, she has to service 70 machines at over 20 locations. Only one is an emergency. A cold-drink machine is leaking in a health club.

Pamela has made the stop at the health club a priority (preye-AHR-ih-tee) on her schedule. When she arrives, she shuts down the machine and uses her master key to open the big door. Right away she sees the problem. The same thing had happened to this machine last month.

Her experience with customers has taught her to be polite when explaining the situation to the manager. "I know you do your best to watch out for vandalism (VAN-duhl-ihz-om). Mr. Walton. But someone has been tampering with the machine again. It's affected the dispensing unit. What can we do as a team to keep this from happening again?"

TALK ABOUT IT

1. Do you think that Pamela is good at what she does? Why or why not? Explain.

2. What kinds of reading do you think Pamela does as a vending machine service worker?

UNDERSTANDING VISUAL INFORMATION

inventory
(IHN-vuhn-tohr-ee) list of supplies on hand including totals

stock items on hand for future sale

For every machine she services, Pamela Canton writes an **inventory** report. She puts the information in a table. This table tells her supervisor how much **stock** is left in the machine when she checks it. This information helps the company decide which products need to be reordered. Read the table and answer the questions that follow it.

SAFE-T VENDING INVENTORY REPORT

LOCATION	PRODUCT				
	Chocolate Bars	Peanut Crackers	Chips	Pretzels	Raisins
Star Gym	50	21	23	10	11
Lo's Car Wash	3	13	20	4	25
Laundry, Etc.	11	11	5	6	8
Grainger, Inc.	14	15	8	9	11
Cedar Glen Apartments	6	26	16	5	0

CHECK YOUR UNDERSTANDING

Circle the correct answer to each question. Base your answers on the report above.

1. Which location had 50 chocolate bars in stock?
   a. Grainger, Inc.   b. Lo's Car Wash   c. Star Gym

2. How many chips were in stock at Laundry, Etc.?
   a. 8   b. 5   c. 16

3. At Grainger, Inc., which product had the lowest number in stock?
   a. chocolate bars   b. chips   c. raisins

4. At which location were there the fewest pretzels in stock?
   a. Star Gym
   b. Lo's Car Wash
   c. Cedar Glen Apartments

Check your answers on page 116.

◆ LESSON WRAP-UP

Workers need to understand visual information on the job. A table presents information in a visual, easy-to-read form. Reading a table is done in two steps:

- First, you read the title to find out what information is being given.
- Then, you read across the rows and down the columns to find the specific information you need.

TITLE		
	COLUMN	**COLUMN**
ROW		
ROW		
ROW		

Because employers need to get as much done in a day as possible, visuals are often used for giving information on the job. Using visuals is the best way to give information briefly in order to get a point across quickly.

It is a good idea to get used to a lot of reading formats. The more practice you have with various types of reading formats, the more skilled a reader you will become.

1. When have you used a table to get information? Did you think it was easy to read and understand? Why or why not?

2. Which parts of a vending machine service job would you like? Which parts do you think you would dislike?

Check your answers on page 116.

UNDERSTANDING VISUAL INFORMATION

49

1. Write a paragraph that compares and contrasts two jobs in the machine trades. For example, what is the same about being a vending machine service worker and an automobile mechanic? What is different?

2. In the chart below, read the causes listed. Then, write in two possible effects for each one. For example, for the first cause, you could write "A cookout might be canceled," or "People carry umbrellas." Use complete sentences.

CAUSE	EFFECT
It's a rainy day.	
You win a million dollars.	
You stay late at work every day one week.	
A friend is very sick.	

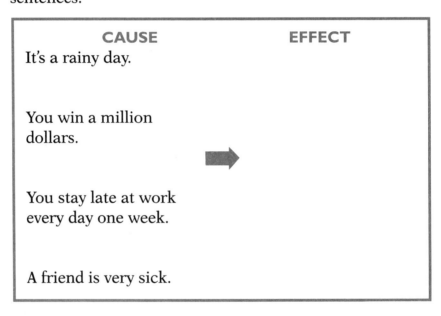

3. Write a paragraph that tells why a worker might quit a job. Remember, the effect is a worker quitting his or her job. You need to write down possible causes. Use only complete sentences.

4. Of the jobs described in this unit—automobile mechanic, machine tool operator, machinist, and vending machine service worker—which one appeals to you most? Why?

Check your answers on page 116.

Structural Work ◆ Occupations ◆

Structural workers build houses, highways, and office and apartment buildings—inside and outside. They include carpenters, painters, carpet installers, bricklayers, and hundreds of other workers. Structural workers must be able to do physical labor for much of the day. They also use thinking and reading skills every day on the job.

As you read the selections in this unit—everything from a business letter to a magazine ad—you will learn important reading skills used in structural work. You also will see how these skills play an important role in any job you may have.

This unit teaches the following reading skills:

◆ making inferences
◆ following directions
◆ distinguishing fact from opinion

You will learn how structural workers use these reading skills in their work.

Working in Plastering

Words to Know

apprenticeship

gypsum

insulation

lathing

masonry

vermiculite

wire-mesh netting

Look around the room where you are sitting. What are the walls and ceilings made of? Although walls and ceilings can be made from many different materials, chances are good that a part of the room is made out of plaster. Plaster is a thick mixture that hardens on drying. It is used to make walls and ceilings.

Like the other jobs in this book, plasterers (PLAS-tuhr-uhrz) need good thinking and reading skills. A plasterer may have to read instructions, product labels, memos, work orders, and even directions to a job site. The better a worker's reading and thinking skills are, the more time and effort he or she can give to doing the job.

Sometimes, information is stated directly in a passage. Other times, you must infer, or "figure out," what is not stated directly. **Making inferences** (IHN-fuhr-uhns-ehz) is the reading skill you'll practice while you learn more about plastering (PLAS-tuhr-ihng).

Job Focus

Plastering is a physical job, but it also involves thinking. Bending, reaching, lifting, and climbing are a major part of the job. A **plasterer** also has to plan ahead, make good choices, and get along with others.

Several years ago, plastering became less popular than other ways of making walls and ceilings. There are faster and cheaper ways. Lately, plastering has become popular again. People want good quality, and plaster lasts longer. Plastering is also a good way to make a room soundproof or fireproof.

By the year 2000, there will be about 30,000 trained plasterers working in this country. Working as an apprentice is a good way to get a job in this field. An apprentice learns the trade from a skilled worker. The Job Corps also offers a one-year course in the basics of plastering.

Making Inferences: How It Works

When you **make an inference,** you make a guess based on clues, or details. Suppose you're in an airport and you see a woman running down the hallway. The woman is holding an airline ticket. She looks worried. When she sees the doors leading to a plane closing, she yells, "No! Wait for me!" What can you infer from the details in this scene?

You could infer, or guess, that the woman was late for her plane. She did not say so directly, but there were many clues to help you figure it out.

The letter below is from the president of the American Plastering Institute. Read the letter below and practice making inferences. Remember to look for clues.

appenticeship
(uh-PREHN-tihs-shihp) time during which someone is learning a trade

October 18

Dear Institute Member:

Thank you for your support over the past year. We should be proud of what this institute has accomplished.

The excitement will begin Friday at 5:30 p.m. Gather with hundreds of other institute members in the Oakwood Ballroom. There will be dinner and first-class entertainment. After dinner, we'll show video highlights of the American Plastering Institute's 50-year history.

Please join us for this important occasion. Tickets are on sale at $75 per couple. All benefits go toward our **apprenticeship** program.

Sincerely,

John H. Alvarez

John H. Alvarez, President

Which of the following can you infer, based on the letter?

a. The American Plastering Institute is holding its last meeting after 50 years in business.

b. The event takes place on a Friday night at 5:30 P.M.

c. The event will celebrate the American Plastering Institute's accomplishments of the past 50 years.

You can infer that *c. the event will celebrate the American Plastering Institute's accomplishments of the past 50 years.* The writer did not state directly that they will celebrate 50 years. But there are many clues that make this a good guess. Note that the second choice is true, but it was not inferred. It is a fact that is stated directly in the letter. The first choice cannot be inferred. There are no clues in the letter that this is a last meeting of the institute.

When you make an inference, you fill in missing information by making what is often called an "educated guess." You combine clues and what you already know, to figure out what is meant. It is almost like solving a puzzle.

Practice making inferences in the example below.

Several men are leaving a high-rise building. They are wearing white workclothes and carrying ladders. Their clothes as well as their faces and arms are spattered with white plaster.

What can you infer about the men?

_____

What are the clues?

_____

_____

You can infer that *the men are plasterers.* The clues are *wearing white workclothes, carrying ladders,* and *spattered with plaster.* You use the clues and what you already know to figure this out.

When you make an inference, be careful not to infer *too much* or incorrectly. For example, when Nathan got to work one day, he saw many workers leaving the job site. He inferred that work was cancelled, and he went home. When he got to work the next day, his supervisor gave him a warning. What happened?

Nathan's inference that work was cancelled was incorrect. In fact, the workers who were leaving the job site were on their way to a meeting. Nathan should have asked if work was cancelled.

Below is a memo listing steps that the supervisor of a job site expects his plaster crew to follow. Read the memo carefully, and then answer the questions that follow.

M E M O

TO: Plaster Crew
FROM: Mike

Follow these steps at <u>every</u> job site:

1. Assemble the following:
   - **gypsum** cement
   - gypsum plaster
   - 1" **wire-mesh netting**
   - Ottawa silica sand

One worker should track supplies, while others bring up supplies from the storage area.

2. Protect all carpeting, tile, and other finished flooring with a waterproof cover. Appliances, windows, and other fixtures should be protected as well.

3. Prepare the site. Electrical outlets should be pulled away and taped to prevent shock. Heating registers should be removed. Removal of plumbing fixtures is optional.

4. Construct **lathing**, one room at a time. First, install a 3/8" metal trim on top of the baseboard. Then, install netting with 6"-centered nails.

5. Mix a base coat of standard gypsum plaster and clean, fine sand in a 1:1 ratio. Apply by hand or machine to a thickness of 1/4" to 5/16".

6. Keep your work areas clean as you go. DO NOT wait to clean up. Be sure that all equipment is kept clean and dry at all times.

---

gypsum (JIHP-suhm) mineral used in making plaster

wire-mesh netting metal screening with holes for holding plaster

lathing (LATH-ihng) series of thin strips of wood or metal used to support plaster for making walls

Answer the following questions based on the memo on page 55.

1. Which of the following can you infer, based on item 1?

   a. Workers need to buy their own materials.
   b. There should be more than one worker on the site.
   c. Gypsum is the best material to use for plastering.
   d. Tracking supplies is the most important part of the job.

2. Which of the following can you infer, based on item 2?

   a. The plastering process is wet.
   b. Flooring is always installed before plastering.
   c. Plastering can be done in the rain.
   d. At least two workers will place a cover down.

3. Which of the following can you infer, based on item 3?

   a. Electricity is installed after plastering is finished.
   b. Leaving plumbing fixtures in is an incorrect step.
   c. It is possible to remove heating registers.
   d. Plumbing fixtures can be ruined by dripping plaster.

4. Which of the following can you infer, based on item 4?

   a. Lathing is the hardest part of the job.
   b. More than one room in a building is being plastered.
   c. The nails to be used are an irregular size and weight.
   d. The metal trim is wider than the baseboard.

5. Which of the following can you infer, based on item 5?

   a. 1/8" plaster is too thin for this job.
   b. More sand is needed than gypsum.
   c. Applying by hand is the best method.
   d. Applying by machine gives the worker better control.

6. Which of the following can you infer, based on item 6?

   a. The supervisor thinks keeping things clean is important.
   b. A different crew is used for cleaning.
   c. Cleanup can be done after the plastering job is complete.
   d. Cleaning supplies must be brought from home.

Check your answers on page 117.

Michele Sorrento is a skilled plasterer. In fact, she is so good at her job that her supervisor often asks her to train apprentices.

"Plastering is a lot more than just spreading a mixture onto walls," says Michele. "The better your mix and the better the lathing you build, the easier it will be to apply the plaster. I tell my apprentices that putting in more time at the front end saves more time by getting the job done right the first time."

"What are some negative things about the job?" one apprentice asks. "Well, to be honest with you, Alex, I've never gotten used to wearing stilts—even after 15 years in this business!" Michele is referring to long poles, attached to footrests. Plasterers often wear these in order to reach ceilings and high walls. "I would rather use a ladder."

Michele continues: "Another downside of this job is how hard it is to get year-round work. No matter how good you are, you'll usually find yourself with some downtime. That's why it's good to pick up other skills like painting and wallpapering."

The part of her job that has surprised Michele the most is the artistic part of plastering. Recently, she worked on a job in which a very old ballroom was being restored. She learned how to make fancy moldings and how to create decorative finishes with plaster. She did a lot of reading about old buildings, and she worked closely with an experienced plasterer who was also a fine artist.

TALK ABOUT IT

1. Does Michele's job interest you? Explain.

2. What can you infer about Michele's plastering job? Discuss your inferences with someone else.

The selection below is taken from a plastering handbook. Read it carefully and answer the questions that follow.

What You Should Know About Fireproofing...

- The disadvantage of steel construction is that, in the event of fire, steel loses its strength as temperature rises.
- Enclosing steel in **masonry** is one way to fireproof it, but this method is expensive and time-consuming.
- When fire breaks out in a closed area, temperatures can reach 1000 degrees in only 5 minutes.
- Lathing and plaster are a good way to fireproof a building.
- Adding **vermiculite** to gypsum instead of adding sand increases **insulation** ability.
- McCormick Place, a huge meeting hall in Chicago, was destroyed by fire—except for the plaster-protected supporting columns, which remained unharmed.

masonry (MAY-suhn-ree) stonework or brickwork

vermiculite (vuhr-MIHK-yuh-leyet) mineral used in insulation and made from expanded mica

insulation (ihn-suh-LAY-shuhn) materials used to prevent passage of heat or cold

CHECK YOUR UNDERSTANDING

Answer the following questions based on the selection above.

1. Which of the following can you infer from the selection?
   a. Steel is a good material to use in building a furnace.
   b. Most of McCormick Place was not built with plaster.
   c. Fireproofing with lathing and plaster is unnecessary.

2. Based on the selection, you can also infer that
   a. a building of steel enclosed in masonry is more fireproof than the same building of lathing and plaster materials.
   b. a small room with closed doors and windows that catches fire can be entered safely within the first 10 minutes.
   c. adding sand to gypsum is dangerous.

3. What main idea can you infer from this selection?
   a. Fireproofing is difficult and expensive.
   b. Use only vermiculite when you work with plaster.
   c. Fireproofing with plaster is very effective.
   d. Steel construction is poor-quality construction.

Check your answers on page 117.

When you make an inference, you "read between the lines." Although something may not be stated directly, you may be able to infer it is true, based on other information.

In this lesson, you learned to use clues to make inferences. You learned to combine clues and what you already know to figure out what is meant. Review what you learned by making inferences based on the example below.

A soccer team dressed in white uniforms walks slowly off the field, heads hanging. Another team dressed in red remains on the field, jumping, yelling, patting each other on the back.

Inference:

Did you infer that *the red team had just beaten the white team in a soccer match*? If you made this inference, you are a great detective! You used the information given as clues to help you read between the lines.

1. Based on what you now know about plastering, what are three inferences you could make about this type of work? Which clues given in the lesson helped you?

2. Tell about a time when you may have inferred *too much* or incorrectly. It could have been a situation with family or friends. Why did it happen? How can you prevent it from happening again?

Check your answers on page 117.

Installing Floor Covering

▼▼▼▼▼▼▼▼▼▼▼▼▼
Words to Know

adhesive

emissions

inspect

nonflammable

occupants

ventilate

A floor covering installer covers wood or concrete floors with materials to give them a "finished" look. A finished floor may be covered in hardwood, carpeting, vinyl sheeting, or tile.

Some flooring is put down with hammer and nails. Other flooring is put down with glue. One flooring company may want workers to use certain tools. Another company may allow workers to use whatever tools they prefer.

In this lesson, you'll learn about the job of floor covering installer. You'll also learn about an important reading skill: **following directions.** As you know, a large part of any job is doing what your employer tells you to do. If you can follow directions well, the chances are good that you will do your job well and satisfy your employer.

Job Focus

Floor covering installation (ihn-stuh-LAY-shuhn) is a physical job. Wood planks, rolls of carpet, and cases of tiles can weigh several hundred pounds. Moving these materials around is hard work. A **floor covering installer** spends lots of time kneeling and squatting on the floor, putting materials in place. Floor covering installers also must be able to work with a partner, measure floors and supplies, and talk to customers.

Jobs for floor covering installers are expected to increase through the year 2005. The more experience a worker has with a variety of floor coverings, the better his or her position will be in the work force. Three-fourths of the over 100,000 floor covering installers in the United States are carpet installers.

Following Directions: How It Works

All of us have followed directions at one time or another in our lives. You may have followed a friend's directions to his or her house. Or you may have followed the directions on a package of taco mix or aspirin. **Following directions** is nothing more than doing a number of tasks correctly in the right order. The directions usually tell you *what, when, where,* and *how (much).*

Read the following checklist for a tile installer. The checklist provides directions to follow for completing a job well.

Qualitex® Tile Installer's Checklist

Customer satisfaction is our most important goal. If you pay attention to these rules, you will earn the respect of the customer and avoid expensive mistakes.

BEFORE THE JOB
1. Review installation plans and resolve any questions about the job.
2. Check your toolbox to make sure you have everything you need. Check for the sketch of the area to be covered.
3. Confirm that you have ordered the correct tile and **adhesives** and that they will be delivered to the job site.

ON THE JOB
4. BE ON TIME!! If you are going to be late, call the customer.
5. Be friendly but show respect at all times. Do not discuss personal problems with the customer. Do not argue with your co-workers.
6. Do not be a "salesperson" on the job. Instead of giving information about the product, ask the customer to call the store with any questions. Never discuss how difficult the tile is to install.

AFTER THE JOB
7. Clean the entire work area. Place trash where the customer tells you to, and mop the tiling.
8. Invite the customer to **inspect** your work with you.

---

adhesive (ad-HEE-sihv) sticky substance used for gluing

inspect (ihn-SPEHKT) look at carefully for errors

If a tile installer follows these directions, he or she will be providing good customer service. Each of the tile installers described below works for Qualitex Tile. Read each paragraph. Decide whether each installer is following company directions.

Duane—The morning he is scheduled to tile a customer's bathroom, Duane gets up early and checks his toolbox. He finds everything he needs, including a detailed drawing of the bathroom floor's measurements. He leaves the house early enough to get to the Kyles' house before the scheduled time of 8:00 A.M. He politely says hello to Mrs. Kyle and heads to the job site.

Clarissa—Late Tuesday afternoon, Clarissa reads on her schedule that she is due at 2300 West Atkins at 7:00 A.M. Wednesday morning. She has been hired to install a new kitchen floor. She calls the company warehouse and confirms that the pale green tile #E45 and adhesive that Mr. Chen ordered has already been dropped off at the site. Before she goes to bed that night, Clarissa checks her tools and supplies one last time. She puts a drawing of the kitchen in her duffle bag.

Ernest—A long-time employee for Qualitex, Ernest arrives at his job site on time Wednesday morning. He has checked his tools, tile supplies, and drawing. All is in order, including confirmation of tile delivery. He says hello to Mr. Pucinski and gets to work tiling the bathroom floor. "I like the tile you chose, Mr. Pucinski," he calls out. "But you probably paid too much. There's a tile that's almost exactly the same thing that sells for a lot less."

Which of the installers followed all the directions?

_____

According to the tile installer's checklist, only *Clarissa* followed all the directions.

What direction did Duane miss? _____

_____

He did not call ahead to confirm that the tile would be at the job site.

What about Ernest? _____

_____

He forgot the important #6 on the list of directions. He should not have discussed prices with the customer.

When you follow directions, pay attention to the details. Understanding the details can make the difference between correctly done work and poorly done work.

Following directions is important in doing a job correctly and safely. When floor covering is installed, dust and chemicals are always present. Most floor installation companies have specific instructions on how to prevent these from harming people.

ventilate (VEHN-tuhl-ayt) allow fresh air in

emissions (ih-MIHSH-uhnz) substances released into the air

nonflammable (nahn-FLAM-uh-buhl) not likely to catch on fire easily

occupants (AHK-yoo-puhnts) people who live in a particular place

Directions to Ensure Indoor Air Quality
CONSUELA CARPET CO., INC.

*Always **ventilate** working rooms with fresh air during all phases of installation. As often as possible, ventilate for at least 72 hours after installation.*

❑ Open as many doors and windows as possible. Use window or exhaust fans to rid air of chemical **emissions**.

❑ Vacuum the old carpeting BEFORE REMOVAL to minimize dust particles.

❑ Vacuum the floor IMMEDIATELY after the old carpeting and cushioning have been removed.

❑ If carpeting is to be glued to the floor, use a low-emitting and **nonflammable** adhesive such as Anton low-VOC.

*Some **occupants** may be especially sensitive to dust and chemicals.*

❑ Advise occupants to leave the premises while carpet is being removed or installed.

❑ Allow the new carpet to "rest" unrolled in a well-ventilated area for a day or more before installation.

❑ Advise occupants to notify a doctor if someone experiences flu-like symptoms that may be caused by the carpet installation.

Answer the following questions based on the Consuela Carpet Co. directions on page 63.

1. Which of the following steps should be taken after carpet installation has been completed, if possible?

    a. leave the premises
    b. vacuum the old carpeting
    c. ventilate the area for at least 72 hours
    d. allow the new carpeting to "rest"

2. It is important to ventilate rooms with fresh air

    a. before new carpeting is delivered.
    b. before old carpeting is removed.
    c. only for occupants who are sensitive.
    d. during all phases of installation.

3. Which of the following steps should be performed first for an occupant who is sensitive?

    a. vacuum the old carpeting
    b. allow the new carpeting to "rest" unrolled
    c. use a low-emitting adhesive
    d. notify a doctor

4. An employee of Consuela Carpet Co. performed the following steps at a job site. If he followed company directions, in what order did he complete the steps? Number from 1 to 6 in the spaces provided.

    _____ He opened two doors and four windows.

    _____ He used Anton low-VOC glue to put down the new carpet.

    _____ He unrolled the new carpeting and left it in a well-ventilated room.

    _____ He vacuumed the floor under the old carpeting.

    _____ He vacuumed the old carpeting.

    _____ He removed the old carpeting.

Check your answers on page 117.

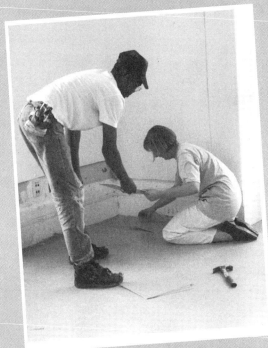

Roberto Cuhn and Jill Stobern are a floor installation team. When Roberto and Jill install vinyl sheeting, such as linoleum (lih-NOH-lee-uhm) they split the job into planning and cutting. Jill explains, "Roberto's great with blueprints, sketches, and customer directions. I help him with drawing and measuring, but I follow his lead. He has a better visual sense than I do, so he's in charge of planning."

"Once we've got the area measured and sketched out," adds Roberto, "Jill takes control. Jill makes a better cutter than I do. She has a terrific eye, and she rarely makes a mistake. I help by holding materials in place and backing her up with the drawings." Throughout their day, Jill and Roberto follow directions. They follow company directions, they follow customer directions, and they follow each other's directions. Some of these directions are spoken, and some are written. "As much as possible, we like to get all directions in writing," says Jill. "It helps to have something to refer to in case a question comes up. Roberto and I usually take directions home with us the day before a job so we can read what we'll need to do the next day."

Roberto chuckles. "Remember the time we arrived at the job site with no directions or work order? We showed up with all our vinyl tools, expecting to be laying down some vinyl tiles in the playroom. Instead, we found 500 square yards of carpeting. That was the last time we tried to work without directions!"

TALK ABOUT IT

1. Why is following directions so important for Roberto and Jill?

2. Think of a time when following directions was important to you. How did you handle the situation? Why was it important to follow these directions?

From time to time, a floor covering installer may be asked to remove a spot from a carpet. Most carpet installers are equipped with a spot-removal guide. Below is an example of such a guide. Look over the guide and answer the questions that follow.

CARPET AND RUG SPOT-REMOVAL GUIDE

To remove a spot, use the cleaners in order until the spot is gone. The cleaners are listed below, a–h. The numbers in the guide tell you which cleaners to use and in what order.

a. Dry cleaning fluid
b. Nail polish remover
c. Detergent solution
d. Warm water

e. White vinegar solution
f. Ammonia solution
g. Spot-removal kit
h. Vacuum

Type of spot	a	b	c	d	e	f	g	h
Grape juice			1	3	2		4	
Grass	2	1	3	6	5	4	7	
Hairspray	3		1	2				
Ink	1		2	5	4	3		
Jam, jelly			1	4	3	2	5	
Lipstick	2	1	3	6	5	4	7	
Makeup	3		1	2				
Markers			1	2				
Milk	1		2	5	4	3		
Oil, car	1		2	4		3		
Orangeade			1	3		2		

CHECK YOUR UNDERSTANDING

Answer the following questions based on the guide above.

1. Suppose you try to remove a makeup spot with a detergent solution, and then you rinse it with warm water. The spot still has not come out. What step should you try next?

2. List the ways to remove a grape juice spot, in the order in which you should try them.

3. There are seven possible ways to remove a grass spot. (Circle the correct answer.)

TRUE   **FALSE**

4. A customer first tried dry cleaning fluid to remove a hairspray spot. Was he following the directions in the guide?

If not, what should he have done first?

Check your answers on page 117.

◆ LESSON WRAP-UP

Following directions is one of the most important skills you'll ever learn. On the job and in your everyday life, you often need to read directions and understand them.

To follow directions well, you have to read and understand details. Directions often include answers to questions such as *what, when, how (much),* and *where.*

In this lesson, you learned that installing floor covering is a job that requires various sets of directions, depending on what the specific task is. For example, gluing tile requires different steps than those for installing carpet. Also, one customer may want leftover materials stored in her basement. Another customer may ask you to take all leftover scraps with you. You can see how important it is to follow directions for each job.

Think of something you know how to do well. It could be something as simple as setting a dinner table or as complex as giving a car a tune-up. Write directions for how to complete this task. Imagine that someone will have to follow these directions, so use lots of details in your writing.

Check your answers on page 117.

Working as a Carpenter's Assistant

▼▼▼▼▼▼▼▼▼▼▼▼

Words to Know

access

contemporary

lattice

pressure-treated

priming

traditional

union

Carpenters do just about everything you can think of that involves wood. They use hand and power tools to build, install, and repair structures. Their jobs range from building stairways to cabinets to entire buildings. Carpentry is physical work. A carpenter climbs, stoops, lifts, and stands to do the job. But carpentry is mental work as well. A carpenter needs to be able to read blueprints, diagrams, directions, and product labels.

It is important for a carpenter's assistant to learn basic facts about carpentry. The assistant may learn that a *buck* is an opening in which a carpenter installs a door or window. The assistant may also learn that oak is a harder wood than pine. Knowing such facts is part of the job.

In this lesson you'll learn to **distinguish fact from opinion.** A fact is something that can be proven true. An opinion is something that a person believes. One carpenter, for example, may think that a Vaughan hammer is the best one to buy. Another carpenter may think that Stanley makes a better hammer. Each is an opinion, not a fact.

Job Focus

The **carpenter's assistant** follows the instructions of a skilled carpenter. The assistant learns by watching the carpenter work.

Carpentry can be divided into two categories: "rough" and "finish." Rough carpenters do the outside work. They build the basic frame of a structure, assembling floor joists, subfloors, walls, and partitions. Finish carpenters do inside work, such as laying floors, building stairs, and installing cabinets. Finish carpenters also do minor repairs.

The outlook for skilled carpenters is good. It is expected that there will be many jobs for carpenters through the year 2000. Currently, there are over one million carpenters at work in the United States. Many belong to unions.

Distinguishing Fact From Opinion: How It Works

It is important to know how to **distinguish fact from opinion.** As you know, a fact is something that can be proven true. An opinion is something that a person believes. It cannot be proven true or false.

Read this ad that appeared in *World of Woodwork* magazine. See if you can point out the facts and the opinions.

contemporary
(kuhn-TEHM-puh-rehr-ee)
current; modern

traditional
(truh-DIHSH-uhn-uhl)
conforming to styles from the past

> ## Gleason Garage Doors Are The Best!
>
> We have 12 styles to choose from. Some designs are **contemporary** and some are **traditional.** Some have windows, and some do not. The wood used is beautiful. Prices start as low as $249.99. Gleason makes the best doors, no matter what the price!

To decide whether each statement is a fact or an opinion, ask yourself: "Can it be proven?" Look closely at each statement made in this ad. Write *fact* next to the statements of fact and *opinion* next to the opinion statements.

"Gleason Garage Doors Are the Best!" _____

If you said this statement is an *opinion*, you are correct. Some people may like the doors, while others may not. You cannot prove that something is the "best."

"We have 12 styles to choose from." _____

If you said that this statement is a *fact*, you are correct. You can count the number of styles made by Gleason.

"Some designs are contemporary, and some are traditional." _____

If you said that this statement is a *fact*, you are correct. Some door styles were created a long time ago but are still used now. Other door styles were recently created.

"Some have windows, and some do not."　　_____

This statement is a *fact*. It can be proven by checking the doors themselves.

"The wood used is beautiful."　　_____

If you said that this statement is an *opinion*, you were correct. Whether something is beautiful or not is a matter of personal taste. People can have different opinions about the beauty of something.

"Prices start as low as $249.99."　　_____

This statement is a *fact* based on the ad.

"Gleason makes the best doors,
no matter what the price!"　　_____

This statement from the ad is an *opinion*. People can have very different ideas about what makes the best door—type of work, quality of work, hardware, and so on.

In the space below, write down a fact about what you look like. Be sure the fact can be proven.

_____

_____

Now write an opinion about how you look. Remember that this is *your opinion* and that someone may disagree with it.

_____

_____

Your fact probably included a number or a color. For example, *I am 5 feet 5 inches tall* or *I have brown eyes*. Your opinion probably was a judgment of some kind; for example, *I look like Fred Flintstone* or *I'm very handsome*.

Remember:
- A fact is something that can be proven to be true. You can verify the truth of a fact.
- An opinion is something that a person believes. An opinion is something you can agree or disagree with.

Here is an article that appeared in a magazine for carpenters. It has facts and opinions about wages and government. Read the article and answer the questions.

union (YOON-yuhn) organization of workers formed to achieve common goals

Union Rallies Against Lower Wages

On July 27, about 400 workers from a local carpenter's **union** marched to the State House to protest a change in wage policy. The average yearly pay for a construction worker is now $28,000. Lawmakers are considering lowering the pay to $22,000.

"A government that would do that to workers is dangerous," said Tom White, a carpenter at the rally. "I have a wife and three small children. A gallon of milk at our local grocery store costs $1.99. Just last month, it was $1.89. I have no money in my savings account."

George Salvatore spoke for the Governor in response to the marchers. "Everybody would like to have higher wages. Transportation workers' average wages have already been lowered 10%. The best way to keep the economy going is to keep wages at a lower average."

CARPENTERS MONTHLY   **26**

CHECK YOUR UNDERSTANDING

Answer the following questions based on the article above.

1. In the first paragraph of the article, all of the statements are opinions. (Circle the correct answer.)

      TRUE   FALSE

2. Which statements made by Tom White are facts?

    a. "A government that would do that to workers is dangerous."
    b. "I have a wife and three small children."
    c. "A gallon of milk at our local grocery store costs $1.99. Just last month it was $1.89."
    d. "I have no money in my savings account."

3. The first sentence in the third paragraph is a fact. (Circle the correct answer.)

TRUE   FALSE

4. Which statement made by George Salvatore is a fact?

Check your answers on page 118.

ON THE JOB

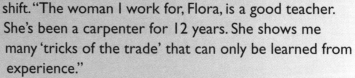

Lisa Fay likes the variety of her job as a carpenter's assistant. She does at least ten different things in her 7:00 A.M. to 3:00 P.M. shift. "The woman I work for, Flora, is a good teacher. She's been a carpenter for 12 years. She shows me many 'tricks of the trade' that can only be learned from experience."

Lisa does a variety of reading on the job. She reads work orders filled out by Flora. She reads the labels on all the carpentry supplies they use. She reads instruction manuals for various power tools. By knowing how to read well, Lisa learns many facts necessary to do her job.

Lisa also reads notes and instructions from customers. "That's when I have to remember the difference between fact and opinion!" she laughs.

"Once, I spent all day installing shelves in a school building. The customer said that I had put them in too high. He wanted me to tear them out. Instead, I checked the work order and showed him the facts. He had asked for 3-foot-high shelving. I used my tape measure to show him that the shelves were, in fact, 3 feet from the floor. He still thought that the shelves looked too high, but that was his opinion. He decided to stick with the facts and leave the shelves where they were. I was really glad that I didn't tear them out right away!"

TALK ABOUT IT

1. Do you think Lisa handled her customer's concern correctly? Explain why or why not.

2. If Lisa did not have good reading skills, what kinds of things might go wrong during her workday? Make a list, and compare it with other students' lists.

Below is a portion of a work order for a carpentry job. It describes the job and how it was supposed to be done. Also below is a customer's memo about the job that was actually done. Read both carefully and answer the questions that follow.

access (AK-sehs) passage; way to get into

pressure-treated (PREHSH-uhr TREET-uhd) processed to prevent warping and other damage

lattice (LAT-ihs) open framework made of interwoven strips of wood

priming (PREYEM-ihng) preparing for painting by applying an undercoat

---

WORK ORDER

JOB: McNally Deck

Description: Build outdoor deck with family room **access**.

Materials: **pressure-treated** lumber for flooring and rails

pine **lattice** work for siding, 1"x4" pine on seams

(**priming**, painting, and staining not included)

Size: deck: $27\frac{1}{2}$ feet by 15 feet
lattice: $3\frac{1}{2}$ feet high

Estimated start date: 5/30/96
Estimated end date: 7/1/96

Date: 6/25/96
   To: Williams & Sons Carpentry
From: Jane Chaus

I have some concerns about the deck you are building for us. Please call me Monday to discuss the situation.

1. You are taking too long to complete the job. My neighbor's deck was built in three weeks. You have been working three weeks and you are not done yet.
2. The lattice work that you installed is 4 feet high. It is higher than I ordered.
3. The deck is too small compared to my neighbor's.

Jane Chaus

Answer the following questions based on the work order and letter on page 73.

1. Which statements in Mrs. Chaus's letter are facts that can be proven?

2. What are Mrs. Chaus's opinions?

3. Was Mrs. Chaus correct in her statement about the lattice? (Circle the correct answer.)

          YES   NO

How do you know?

4. What were the measurements of the deck supposed to be?

5. How can the carpenters prove that the deck size is correct?

Check your answers on page 118.

◆ LESSON WRAP-UP

Whether you are at your job or elsewhere, being able to distinguish fact from opinion is important. Have you ever heard the saying, "Don't believe everything you read"? This is a good rule to remember.

Remember:
- A fact is something that can be proven true.
- An opinion is something that a person believes.

1. Suppose a co-worker writes a note to you saying, "You've been working too hard all day; you should take a break." What might happen if you mistook this opinion for an actual fact?

2. Suppose your supervisor sends you a memo stating: "The boards you cut today are 6 inches too short." What might happen if you thought, "Oh, that's just his opinion"?

Check your answers on page 118.

1. Write a paragraph that gives an example of someone making an inference.

2. Give directions on how to get from your home to a grocery store. Be sure to be specific and use lots of details so that anyone can follow what you have written!

3. Choose one of the jobs described in this unit. Write one paragraph that gives your opinion about the job. Then write another paragraph that gives some facts about the same job.

OPINION:

FACT:

Check your answers on page 118.

Unit Four

· Bench Work Occupations ·

Bench work jobs are carried out at a worktable that is set in place in a plant or shop. Bench workers use their hands to fit, grind, assemble, finish, or repair small objects and materials. In this unit, you will look at three types of bench work jobs: furniture manufacturing, locksmithing, and jewelry making and repair. Each of these jobs, like all bench work jobs, requires the ability to do detailed work with the hands. Bench work is the type of work that cannot be done by machines. This work requires a person to work closely with small parts and with tools.

As you work through this unit, you will gain greater skill in understanding what you read. You will see how bench workers use what they read to draw conclusions, solve a problem, and classify information. The office memos, repair manuals, and ads in this unit are examples of on-the-job reading that bench workers do every day.

This unit teaches the following reading skills:

◆ drawing conclusions
◆ drawing conclusions to solve a problem
◆ classifying information

You will learn how bench workers use these reading skills in their work.

77

Making Wood Furniture

Most wood furniture (FER-nuh-chuhr) is made in factories. There are three basic steps that wood goes through in a furniture factory. These steps involve working (or shaping), assembling, and finishing.

Think about all the pieces of furniture you have at home. Then think about all the other furniture you've seen in offices, schools, buildings, and stores. If you recognize that there is a large amount of furniture bought and sold, you can safely draw the conclusion that making furniture is a big business.

Drawing conclusions is an important skill you use every day. When you draw conclusions, you use the given information and what you already know to come up with new ideas. For example, by thinking about all the furniture in your home and all around you, you may have concluded that making furniture is a big business. This is a good example of drawing a conclusion.

Job Focus

Wood planks, dried for several months, arrive at the furniture factory. **Woodworking machine operators** saw, sand, mold, and carve the wood into furniture parts. **Assemblers** (uh-SEHM-blers) put the parts together, using power tools, nails, glue, and their hands. **Finishers** use sandpaper to smooth the wood. They also apply stains (staynz), paints, and polishes to give the wood a finished look.

About 165,000 people are employed as furniture workers. As the state of the economy rises and falls, so do furniture sales. However, people will always be needed to replace workers who leave their jobs due to retirement or other reasons.

Drawing Conclusions: How It Works

To **draw a conclusion,** you use the details that are given and information you already know to make a new observation or decision. Some materials you read may provide you with a conclusion in the form of a judgment, a summary, or an opinion. Other times, you may have to draw your own conclusions.

Below is an article about an anti-pollution (puh-LOO-shun) study. The article appeared in a magazine for furniture factories. Read the article and draw your own conclusions.

Boles Manufacturing Chosen for Anti-Pollution Study

The state Pollution Control department has chosen Boles Manufacturing to take part in its new study. Over 100 companies applied to take part in the study. Boles was selected based on its reputation for obeying local laws that protect the environment.

The goal of the study is to find new ways to apply furniture finishes—**stains**, **varnishes**, and polishes. Researchers are looking for ways to reduce air pollution during furniture finishing. The results of the study will be published by the state government. Officials hope that furniture factories in this state will help reduce air pollution by changing their finishing processes.

Boles has been making furniture for over 40 years. Don Dowling, president of the company, spoke at a recent press conference: "We are proud to have been selected for this study. We are concerned about the air quality in our state, and we are committed to doing all that we can to improve it."

4   Making Furniture

---

stains (staynz) liquids that changes the color of wood

varnishes (VAHR-nihsh-uhs) colorless, oil-based paints that dry and leave a thin, hard, glossy finish

Which of the following conclusions can you draw, based on the information in the article? Choose two.

    a. Boles is being forced by the state to take part in the study.

    b. Boles is a very responsible company.

    c. The study may produce a new way of applying stain or varnish that does not pollute the environment.

If you said that *b. Boles is a very responsible company* and that *c. The study may produce a new way of applying stain* or *varnish that does not pollute the environment*, you drew good conclusions. The first conclusion is based on the information that many companies had applied to take part in the study and that Boles was selected based on its reputation. The second conclusion is based on the information related to the goal of the anti-pollution study.

When you draw a conclusion, make sure you have the facts to back it up. Have you ever heard of "jumping to conclusions"? When you jump to a conclusion, you disregard or misread necessary facts and come up with a false conclusion.

For example, can you conclude that Don Dowling has been the president of Boles for over 40 years? No, you can't. Boles has been making furniture for over 40 years, and Don Dowling is the president now. However, these facts do not suggest that he has been the president for all those years.

Below is a safety poster about chemicals used in furniture finishing. Read the safety poster and answer the questions that follow.

linseed (LIHN-seed) **oil** oil extracted from pressed seeds of the flax plant

---

FURNITURE FINISHING SAFETY

☞ **What is spontaneous combustion?**
Spontaneous combustion (spahn-TAY-nee-uhs kum-BUS-chun) is a chemical reaction that produces a sudden fire without any igniting element.

☞ **What can cause the heat?**
Oil finishes containing **linseed oil** are chemicals that give off heat when processed.

☞ **What is the danger?**
If oil-soaked rags are piled up, enough heat will build up to cause spontaneous combustion.

☞ **What's the best way to avoid the danger?**
Handle all chemicals carefully. Put oil-soaked rags, brushes, and paper in a metal container filled with water. Immediately seal the container.

☞ **Where should the container be stored?**
Carry the container, labeled, to the fenced area outside the factory building. The waste team will dispose of it according to local regulations.

LESSON 10 ◆ MAKING WOOD FURNITURE

Answer the questions based on the safety poster on page 80.

1. Which of the following conclusions can you draw from the poster?

   a. Furniture factory workers are careless.
   b. Linseed oil is a poor choice for furniture finishing.
   c. Safety is an important concern for furniture factories.
   d. All furniture finishing should be done outdoors.

2. Which of the following is the best conclusion to draw about oil-soaked rags, based on the safety poster?

   a. They are safest when piled outside.
   b. They are dangerous unless they are sealed in a water-filled container.
   c. They are dangerous when placed close to a flame.
   d. They are used repeatedly in furniture finishing.

3. A worker from a furniture factory is carrying a covered metal can out of the building. The can is labeled "OIL RAGS." Which of the following is the best conclusion to draw?

   a. The worker has purchased new factory supplies.
   b. The worker is stealing company property and should be stopped.
   c. The worker is a member of the waste team disposing of dangerous chemicals.
   d. The worker is properly storing the used oil rags.

4. Suppose you are ending your shift at the furniture factory. You pass by a friend's workstation, and you see some rags piled up under his bench. What should you do?

   a. Hit the alarm button, since a fire is about to start.
   b. Make certain that the rags are clean and do not contain any oil finishes.
   c. Assume that your friend has taken all safety precautions and leave the rags where they are.
   d. Throw the rags away if they are dirty.

Check your answers on page 119.

Charlie Burns works as a finisher at a large furniture factory. His workstation has a bench facing the roller-based assembly line. As each bookcase rolls down the line, Charlie latches it to his bench and begins work.

The bookcases usually come to Charlie after their final sanding. The surfaces have been smoothed and are ready for stain and varnish. The bookcases, which measure about 4 feet high and 3 feet wide, usually need to be wiped down with a soft cloth to remove any fine dust particles.

At the beginning of his shift, Charlie read the order form for this particular run of bookcases. This form specified what finishes the bookcases would need. In his job, Charlie is responsible for making sure that the stain is mixed to produce the correct finish.

"This morning's run is about 200 pine bookcases," Charlie says. "They'll be stained a dark chocolate brown, and then varnished. Our company procedures require me to run a test on scrap wood from the same batch as the bookcases. I'll spray some stain on it, let it dry, then take it over to the varnish station. The test scrap has to be approved by my supervisor before we can begin the run. Just because the stain looked right on yesterday's batch of bookcases doesn't mean it'll look the same on today's. That's a conclusion you just can't jump to in this work."

TALK ABOUT IT

1. List some conclusions you can draw about Charlie and his job at the furniture factory, based on this selection.

2. What aspects of Charlie's job appeal to you? What parts of his job would you not enjoy?

Companies sometimes conduct a survey (SER-vay) by asking people questions. The survey tells what customers are thinking. The company then draws conclusions about what type of product to make.

The chart below shows the results of a survey done by a large furniture company. The company printed the survey results in its company newsletter. The newsletter explained that 70% meant 70 out of 100 people, 95% meant 95 out of 100 people, and so on. Read the chart and answer the questions that follow.

particle board
(PAHR-tih-kuhl bawrd) man-made board made from small pieces of wood that are bonded together

veneer (vuh-NEER) thin layer of fine wood glued to plywood or particle board to give the look of solid wood

Youngsville County Furniture, Inc.
Survey Results

QUESTION ASKED	YES	NO
1. Do you prefer country styling over contemporary styling?	70%*	30%
2. Do you prefer solid wood over **particle board?**	95%	5%
3. Would you be willing to pay more for solid wood than for particle board?	80%	20%
4. Do you prefer solid wood over **veneer?**	90%	10%
5. Would you be willing to pay more for solid wood than veneer?	80%	20%
6. Have you ever purchased "youth-size" furniture?	10%	90%
7. Would you be willing to pay extra for cedar-lined drawers and cabinets?	30%	70%

8. Which do you consider the most beautiful of all woods?

Mahogany	40%	Cherry	25%
Oak	20%	Maple	10%
Pine	5%		

9. How often do you buy new furniture?

once/month	5%	twice/year	10%
once/year	30%	once/3 years	55%

* 70 percent (70%) means 70 out of 100 people.

Answer the following questions based on the survey on page 83.

1. Based on responses to question 1, which of the following is the best conclusion?

    a. Country-style furniture is expensive.
    b. Contemporary-style furniture is unattractive.
    c. Country furniture is a popular style.

2. What can you conclude about what people think about quality?

    a. People are willing to pay more for quality wood.
    b. People love a bargain.
    c. Veneer products do not sell well.

3. Based on the responses to question 6, which of the following is the best conclusion?

    a. Children do not need furniture.
    b. Making youth-size furniture is a good business decision.
    c. People do not consider youth-size furniture to be necessary.

4. Based on the responses to question 7, which of the following is the best conclusion?

    a. Lining drawers and cabinets with cedar is not a good decision for a furniture company.
    b. Cedar lining makes drawers and cabinets smell better.
    c. Cedar lining is very expensive.

5. Suppose you own a furniture company and you have been told you can buy a truckload of mahogany or a truckload of pine for the same price. Your goal is to make furniture that will sell. Which kind of wood would you buy? Why?

6. What can you conclude based on the responses to question 9?

Check your answers on page 119.

◆ LESSON WRAP-UP

Drawing conclusions involves making observations or decisions based on all the facts you can gather. The more information you have, the easier it is to draw a conclusion. Try this exercise yourself or with a partner.

Read the statements and conclude what Howard's job is.

Howard woke up at 7:00 A.M. to get ready for work.

It's impossible to conclude what job Howard has with this little information. Now let's add a fact:

He put on boots, overalls, and a toolbelt.

Now you know a little more about Howard's job. However, since there are many jobs that require tools, you cannot draw a conclusion yet. Let's add some more information.

When he arrived at the factory, his supervisor told him to work on an order for 75 coffee tables.

By now, you have some ideas about Howard's job. But can you be sure? Read the last statement below. Use what you have learned about furniture making to conclude what Howard's job is.

Howard went to his workstation and checked the settings on his power sander.

You can make a fairly good guess that Howard is a furniture sander at a large factory. Can you see that the more information you have, the better your conclusion?

1. List some facts about a job. Read the facts one at a time to a partner. Let him or her practice drawing conclusions by guessing what the job is based on your facts.

2. Have you ever "jumped to a conclusion" before you had all the facts? Explain what happened and why.

Check your answers on page 119.

Working as a Locksmith

▼▼▼▼▼▼▼▼▼▼▼

Words to Know

bittings

blank key

code

combination lock

impression

lockpick

tumbler

People depend on locks to keep themselves, their families, and their possessions safe. As you know, locks can be found in homes and cars, as well as in offices, banks, factories, and other businesses. There are hundreds of kinds of locks to fill various needs.

Locksmiths install, change, and repair locks. They also open locked doors and make new keys or extra keys. Some highly skilled locksmiths design and install master key systems and electronic (ih-lehk-TRAHN-ihk) security (sih-KYOOR-ih-tee) systems.

In many ways, a locksmith can be considered a "problem-solver." Suppose, for example, that a customer has locked his keys in his car. A locksmith will be called in to solve the problem in the best way possible.

As you learn more about locksmithing, you'll also focus on an important reading skill—**drawing conclusions.** You will learn that when you find a solution to a problem, you are drawing a conclusion based on all the information you have. This is an important skill, no matter what kind of work you do.

Job Focus

Locksmiths work either on their own or for a locksmith company. Work is sometimes done in a workshop and sometimes on-site—where the lock is actually located. Locksmiths perform very detailed tasks with small parts. So they need to have excellent vision and hand-eye coordination (koh-awr-dn-AY-shuhn). Because they are involved in people's security, locksmiths also must be very honest.

The employment outlook for locksmiths is excellent. As more people want greater protection against theft and injury, more and more locksmiths will be needed. Skilled locksmiths who keep up to date on new security systems are hardly ever without work.

Drawing Conclusions: How It Works

combination (kahm-buh-NAY-shuhn) **lock** lock that is opened by turning a dial to specific numbers in a certain order

impression (ihm-PREHSH-uhn) mark made on the surface of a blank key

bittings (BIHT-ihngs) the cuts and jags in the shaft of a key

blank key key without bittings cut in it

code letters and numbers in a manual that identify a type of key

lockpick tool that opens a lock

Think about the typical work day of a locksmith. A customer might bring into the store a **combination lock** that does not work properly. When making a new key for a house or vehicle lock by **impression**, the **bittings** might not show up clearly enough on the **blank key** to make just the right grooves. With this information the locksmith must **draw a conclusion** about how to solve each problem.

When people lock their keys in their car, they often call a locksmith to help them. Read the following page from a locksmith's training manual. As you read, see what problems are identified and what solutions are suggested.

Automobile Lockout Steps

Here are some lockout steps. Be sure to first try the methods that will be the least damaging to the car. If necessary, move on to more forceful solutions. Here is the recommended order of steps:

1. Check the key **code** and make a new key.
2. Use a **lockpick** to open the vehicle door.
3. Use an under-the-window tool.
4. Use a blank key and make an impression.
5. Drill the lock.

Lockout Solutions   5

The manual gives five possible solutions to the automobile lockout problem. But the manual suggests that the locksmith try the solutions in the order given. Read the following situations and try to identify each problem. Then draw a conclusion about how to solve the problem, using the information above.

Mary, a locksmith for Locks, Etc., gets a call from a woman who locked her keys in a 1989 Buick Regal. Mary checks her code book and does not find the correct code to make a new key. What should the locksmith do?

Solution: _____

tumbler (TUHM-bler)
cylinder of the lock that
holds pins in place

An emergency call comes in to Locks, Etc. Someone has locked his keys in a car, but the car model is not known. Without the model name, Mary cannot use her code book. She arrives at the scene and tries to use a lockpick to open the door. However, she finds that the **tumbler** is jammed. What should the locksmith do?

Solution: _____

A woman calls Locks, Etc. She is very upset because she has just dropped her car keys down a city sewer. Her car doors are locked. She says she has no spare key at home. The woman is too upset and confused to identify the model and year of her car. What should the locksmiths do?

Solution: _____

For the first customer, Mary concludes that *a lockpick and an under-the-window tool would probably solve the problem.* In case these tools do not work, she should also *have whatever tools she needs to make a key impression.*

A lockpick did not work for the second customer. Mary concludes that *she should try an under-the-window tool next.*

The third customer has a larger problem than the first two. She has no access to her keys, even if she could get into her car. Therefore, the first three solutions listed in the manual would not help. Mary concludes that *she should make a new key by impression.*

Mary arrives at an emergency lockout scene. Car keys and a one-year-old baby are locked in the car. The parents are very worried about the child. The manual recommends using the least forceful method of entry, which would require Mary to go back to the shop and make a key by code. What should the locksmith do?

Solution: _____

In this case, there is a bigger problem than a basic lockout. Because there is a child involved, rather than waste time making a key, Mary concludes that *she should use a lockpick or an under-the-window tool to get into the car.* Or *she should use the drill if they don't work.*

Of course, solutions to problems cannot always be found in a manual. Many times you'll have to use the information you have to draw your own conclusion and solve the problem.

People who work in the same industry often form groups, associations, or unions. These groups work to keep members informed about what is happening in their industry. Many of these groups publish their own newsletters or magazines for their members. The letter below was written to the editor of a locksmithing newsletter. Read it carefully, and then answer the questions that follow.

October 1

Dear Editor,

This letter is about a problem.

I don't think locksmiths in this region are preparing themselves for the future. We cannot sit back and enjoy business the way we used to. We need to offer more classes in locksmithing. Our members need to improve their skills. We should hold more meetings to share ideas. We should refer customers to each other, and recommend our members' products to each other.

The problem with these ideas, many of you will say, is that they take too much time and money. Classes cost money. Meetings cost money. Time at classes and meetings takes away from time earning money on the job. However, I think there is a solution to these problems. Think about the future. Paying $200 to attend a class might take a bite out of a savings account. But, a locksmith may be able to earn ten times as much by using the new skills learned in a class.

We need to keep on top of what is happening in the world of locksmithing. Let's work together.

Sincerely,

Tom Yun

Tom Yun, member AALA

Answer the questions based on the letter on page 89.

1. What problem does the writer of the letter identify?

    a. Most locksmith classes are too expensive.
    b. Locksmiths are not staying informed about the industry.
    c. He sees things differently from everybody else.
    d. Nobody is recommending the products he sells.
    e. Locksmiths should hold more conferences and meetings.

2. Which of the following solutions does the writer conclude would solve the problem? (More than one answer is possible.)

    a. Raise money to build the local organization.
    b. Offer more locksmithing classes.
    c. Sell more members' products.
    d. Hold more meetings.
    e. Charge less for locksmith classes.
    f. Work longer days.

3. Suppose a new locksmith class is offered at the local community college. According to the writer of this letter, why might some people find it a problem to attend the class? (More than one answer is possible.)

    a. It costs too much money.
    b. There's nothing new to learn.
    c. The location is not convenient.
    d. It would take too much time away from work.
    e. Working together is not of interest for locksmiths.

4. What solution does Tom Yun offer to those people who say they don't want to spend time and money learning new things? Do you agree or disagree with his conclusions? Why?

Check your answers on page 119.

"People think that a locksmith just goes around picking locks open. But that's not all I do," says Mr. Miagi. "It's true that a good part of my day is spent helping people get in somewhere or something. I wear a beeper all day, and it still amazes me how many times people call me. One day this month, I was called to open a safe in someone's home, three cars in the mall parking lot, two apartments, and a safety deposit box at the bank. And this was on a day that I had about eight hours of work to do at the shop!"

Mr. Miagi has been locksmithing for two years. He used to work as a watch repairperson, but he decided that he would be more satisfied working with locks. He enjoys the problem-solving aspects of locksmithing, and he likes helping people feel safe. He also knows that he is good with his hands. "Manual dexterity (dehk-STEHR-ih-tee) or skill in using your hands, is important in this work. I use small tools all day long. Think about how small the bittings need to be on a key that might fit a small suitcase!"

As a locksmith for a 20-employee company, Mr. Miagi spends some of each work day making keys. He is one of the best in the shop at making keys by impression. This involves putting a blank key into the lock. As the blank key is removed, it is marked slightly where the bittings should go. Mr. Miagi then files bittings into the blank until it fits the lock perfectly.

At his workbench each day, Mr. Miagi may have ten or fifteen keys to make, several locks to repair, and some combination locks to work on. "Each job is a little different," he says. "I look at each piece as a problem to solve."

TALK ABOUT IT

1. Have you ever been locked out of your home or car? Explain how you solved the problem.

2. Have you ever had to look in a book to find the solution to a problem? Describe what happened and what the solution was.

Sometimes, a solution to a problem can be found by using the right tool or equipment. The advertisements (ad-vuhr-teyez-muhnts) or ads below are found in a locksmithing magazine. Read each one and answer the questions that follow.

A  Is your key cutter dull? Don't throw it out. You may not know that any cutter model can be sharpened up to 3 or 4 times in its lifetime.
Call
Benson Tools
@ *555-1000.*

B ## Slider-Lock
is a new easy-to-install guard for sliding doors and windows. Your customer can install one quickly and easily—no tools or professional required. For more information on where you can buy
Slider-Locks,
call 1-800-555-0000.

C If your car-entry manual is out of date, buy **Expert Entry Systems**. This manual is updated every year to provide you with easy-to-follow opening methods for every make of car. Comes in a waterproof binder. Handy index included. Write:
Car Systems,
1620 East 10th Street, Mitford, PA

D **Laser-engraved padlocks** now available at Kitco. These high-quality locks are permanently marked with easy-to-read, non-removable lettering. Markings are clean and clear and available in many styles. Call
KITCO
at 1-800-555-1000

E ## DP-45 Spray
lubricates and protects all locking mechanisms.

Great for locks, hinges, sliding doors!

A 15-ounce can is available at your hardware store now for only $2.99.

F ## Flex-Lite
fits where other lights won't go. Incredibly bright bulb; only 1/8 inch diameter.

Don't be in the dark on your next job.

CHECK YOUR UNDERSTANDING

Read the information from the ads and the information given below. Then draw a conclusion about which product would solve the problem. Write the letter of the ad that solves the problem. If there is no product to solve the problem, write "none" in the blank.

1. **Problem:** A customer wants to put a lock on her sliding patio doors. She does not have time to schedule an installation appointment.

Solution:

2. **Problem:** Customers have been complaining that the engravings you've done on their padlocks have been wearing off. They can barely be read after a year or so.
Solution:

3. **Problem:** Your shop is out of good-quality lubricant, or oil, to use on stuck locks.
Solution:

4. **Problem:** The shop's master key cutter isn't working right. You've had it sharpened 5 times already.
Solution:

5. **Problem:** The car-entry manual you've been using does not have the latest model foreign cars listed.
Solution:

Check your answers on page 119.

◆ LESSON WRAP-UP

If you are able to handle problems calmly and effectively, you'll most likely be successful at school, and on the job.

Is your supervisor not satisfied with your work? Is there a machine that is not working properly? Is a customer complaining about something? You need to find out as much information as you can before you can draw any conclusions about what to do.

Once you have identified exactly what the problem is, then it is time to work toward a solution. Reading a guide or manual will help you. Talking to your co-workers and your supervisor is also a good strategy.

1. Identify a problem you've been having for a while. It could be on the job, or at school.

2. Make a list of possible solutions for your problem.

Check sample answers on page 119.

Making and Repairing Jewelry

▼▼▼▼▼▼▼▼▼▼▼▼

Words to Know

cubic zirconium

gauge

pliers

prototype

solder torch

Fine jewelry is made of gold, platinum, or silver. These precious metals are usually set with pearls or gems such as diamonds and rubies. Costume jewelry is made of non-precious metals and imitation stones.

Today, more and more jewelry is made with casts, molds, and stamps in factories. There are hundreds of tools, machines, and supplies used in making jewelry. Picture for a moment the workbench of a jewelry maker. Stored here are tools for cutting, polishing, stamping, soldering (SAHD-uhr-ihng), and engraving (ehn-GRAY-vihng). Also stored are materials for cleaning, polishing, and protecting the jewelry. As you can imagine, it is very important for jewelry makers to keep materials at the workbench well organized.

When you read, it is important to keep information organized as well. Some information you read may be central to understanding the reading. Other information may be interesting but less important. Some things you read may be facts; some may be opinions. In this lesson, you'll learn about **classifying**, or organizing, **information.** *Classifying* means "grouping related information together."

Job Focus

Working as a **jewelry maker** or **repairer** requires excellent hand-eye coordination (koh-awr-duh-NAY-shuhn). The work also requires a lot of attention to detail. Jewelry makers and repairers have to work with tiny pieces, which some people find difficult to do. Jewelry-making tasks can be repetitive. Sometimes, there is the opportunity to be creative at smaller job sites.

The outlook for employment in the jewelry industry is

good. There will be many jobs for workers who have experience with a wide range of materials.

Classifying Information: How It Works

Suppose you work as a jewelry maker. Your supervisor asks you to send her a memo about what supplies you need. You go through your workbench and jot down these supplies: grade 240 sandpaper, round nose pliers, grade 600 sandpaper, borax cone, solder torch fuel, curved point tweezers, beeswax, 20-gauge sterling silver.

When you write your memo, you want it to be easily understood. So you decide to **classify the information**. In other words, you put similar items together in groups. Here is the memo:

To: Nan Rose
From: _____
Date: July 31

Here are the supplies I'll be needing:

<u>Right away:</u> borax cone, **solder torch** fuel, curved point tweezers

<u>By the beginning of next week:</u> 20-**gauge** sterling silver, grade 240 sandpaper

<u>By the end of the month:</u> round-nose **pliers,** grade 600 sandpaper, beeswax

Thank you.

---

solder (SAHD-uhr) **torch** tool that joins or mends metal parts by melting with heat

gauge (gayj) measurement made according to a certain standard

pliers (PLEYE-uhrz) small pinchers for bending, twisting, or holding things

Classifying, or grouping, information makes the memo easier to follow. How are the supplies grouped?

_____

_____

In this memo, the supplies are grouped based on when they are needed. Another way to group the supplies would be to divide them into the steps of the jewelry-making process: creating a mold and **prototype,** heating the metal, making the piece, and polishing.

prototype (PROH-tuh-teyep) first model of something, upon which later examples are based

There is usually more than one way to classify information. When you classify information, first decide what the pieces of information have in common. Then decide the most useful way to classify them.

A worker in a small jewelry shop spends part of her day talking to customers. In addition, part of her day is spent repairing jewelry, and part of her day is spent making new jewelry. Her schedule for one day is shown below. Read the schedule and answer the questions that follow.

Daily Tasks	Monday, June 8
9:00 A.M.	explained our cleaning and polishing system to a customer
9:10 A.M.	began work repairing Mrs. Olsen's chain
9:50 A.M.	answered customer calls
10:10 A.M.	finished Mrs. Olsen's chain repair
11:00 A.M.	began wax mold for opal rings
1:00 P.M.	repaired and polished remaining customer orders
2:30 P.M.	worked on opal ring mold
4:10 P.M.	injected sterling silver into mold
5:00 P.M.	began setting opals
6:00 P.M.	repaired Mr. Sullivan's watch

CHECK YOUR UNDERSTANDING

Classify the above information by putting the worker's tasks in the appropriate groups.

Talking to Customers	Repairs	New Jewelry
1.	3.	7.
2.	4.	8.
	5.	9.
	6.	10.

11. Of what benefit do you think it would be to classify a worker's time?

Check your answers on page 120.

LESSON 12 ◆ MAKING AND REPAIRING JEWELRY

People are often surprised to hear that Gail works for a jewelry maker. Why? Because she wears very little jewelry herself. "People assume that if you work with jewelry, you'll wear a lot of it," Gail explains. "Actually, I wear jewelry only once in a while. When I do, they're very small, very simple pieces."

Gail works as a jewelry finisher in a small factory. Depending on what the orders are that day, she may operate the stamping machine, or work on the polishing station, or do some engraving. "In many ways," says Gail, "I think of myself as a metal worker or craftsperson. People think of a jewelery maker, and they think of someone creating beautiful designs for people to wear. I actually don't do any design at all. I'm given a prototype and a mold, and I just reproduce what I see."

Sound easy? Gail laughs, "It's far from easy. Metal can be very hard to work with. You've got to get it heated to just the right temperature and keep it at that temperature while you work on it. I have to know how to use dozens of tools at just the right time. It gets tricky."

The amount of information Gail has to work with on just one order can be very impressive. Orders list not only materials and amounts. They also request certain textures, finishes, paint applications (ap-lih-KAY-shuns) , and polishing techniques (tehk-NEEKS). "It would be one thing if I could just make what I think looks good," says Gail. "But people have different tastes in jewelry, and my job is to make what *they* like, not what *I* like."

TALK ABOUT IT

Think about what you would like about Gail's job. Then think about what you would not like. Make a chart to classify the information into two groups—Things I Would Like and Things I Would Not Like. Discuss the results with someone else.

cubic zirconium
(KYOO-bihk zuhr-KOH-nee-uhm) lustrous gray-white metallic element used as a substitute for diamonds

There is an ongoing debate in the jewelry industry. The debate is about fine jewelry versus costume jewelry. What are the advantages of each? What are the disadvantages of each? The articles below appeared in a jewelery magazine. Read them and think about how you might classify the information given.

The Virtues of Costume Jewelry

Why pay for fine jewelry when you can get the same look for a lot less money? Costume jewelry is inexpensive and looks just like the real thing. Who besides a jeweler can tell the difference between **cubic zirconium** and a real diamond? When you buy costume jewelry, you can buy a lot of it. So you can always have jewelry that matches your outfit and mood. Fine jewelry is too expensive. You have to polish it all the time, or it looks like junk. Because it's so expensive, you always have to wear the same few pieces, which can be boring. Costume jewelry is the way to go.

Fine Jewelry—The Best Bet!

Fine jewelry will always have value. Unlike imitations, real gold and silver and real gems never become old. They just become more and more valuable. Fine jewelry does not break like costume jewelry does, so it does not need to be replaced—ever. Of course, fine jewelry looks and feels better than imitations. There is no mistaking the appearance and texture of a solid gold bracelet or a diamond ring. Costume jewelry contains all kinds of metal by-products which can irritate the skin. Fine jewelry will be a pleasure to wear for generations to come.

CHECK YOUR UNDERSTANDING

Classify the information above by filling in the chart below.

	Advantages	Disadvantages
Costume Jewelry		
Fine Jewelry		

Check your answers on page 120.

◆ LESSON WRAP-UP

Classifying information is putting information into meaningful groups. When you put information in groups, it is easier to read and understand.

To put information into groups, first decide what each piece of information has in common with other pieces of information. Next, think about why some pieces are different from other pieces. Then you will begin to see how you might classify all the information.

There are many ways to group the words listed below. See if you can classify the words into three groups. Write a title for each group. The first one has been done for you.

large	gold	ruby	red
silver	three	tiny	sapphire
round	two	four	square
oval	diamond	eight	ten

Title: Appearance	Title:	Title:

Now make your own list of 15 words for a partner to classify. You might try to list words from these groups: furniture, jewelry, handtools, or machines. Or choose groups of your own.

Group:	Group:	Group:

Check your answers on page 120.

1. Of the jobs described in this unit, which one appeals to you least? Why? Be specific in your answer.

2. What do you think is the most difficult part of being a jewelry maker? Tell how you came to this conclusion.

3. Suppose you are a worker at a furniture factory and you notice a problem. You have seen some co-workers not following safety rules. What conclusions can you draw to solve this problem? Describe one or two solutions, and tell why you think they would work.

4. Why is it important to have information organized on the job? What might happen if information were not organized?

Check your answers on page 120.

RESPELLING GUIDE

Use the following guide to help you pronounce long and hard words.

Sound	Respelling	Example of Respelling
a as in hat	a	hat
a as in day, date, paid	ay	day, dayt, payd
vowels as in far, on, bother, hot	ah	fahr, ahn, BAH-thuhr, haht
vowels as in dare, air, heir	ai	dair, air, air
vowels as in saw, call, pore, door	aw	saw, kawl, pawr, dawr
e as in pet, debt	eh	peht, deht
e as in seat, beef, chief, **y** as in beauty	ee	seet, beef, cheef BYOO-tee
vowels as in learn, urn, fur, sir	er	lern, ern, fer, ser
i as in sit, bitter, **ee** as in been	ih	siht, BIHT-uhr, bihn
i as in mile, **ei** as in height	eye	meyel, heyet
o as in go	oh	goh
vowels as in boil, toy	oi	boil, toi
vowels as in how, out, bough	ow	how, owt, bow
vowels as in up, come	u	up, kum
vowels as in use, use, bureau, few	yoo	yooz yoose, BYOO-roh, fyoo
vowels as in look, put, foot	oo	look, poot, foot
vowels as in bitter, action	uh	BIHT-uhr, AK-shuhn

Consonants are respelled as they sound. Here are a few examples.

c as in cat	k	kat
c as in dance	s	dans
ch as in Christmas	k	KRIHS-muhs
g as in gem	j	jehm
s as in laser	z	LAY-zuhr
ph as in phone	f	fohn

RESOURCES

The following organizations and publications may provide more information about the jobs covered in this book.

United States Government
U.S. Department of Labor, Employment and Training Administration

Adult Training Programs include the following:
Job Training Partnership Act (JTPA)
This program provides job training for disadvantaged adults who face significant employment barriers. For more information, write:

   Office of Employment and Training
   Programs, Room N4469
   U.S. Department of Labor
   200 Constitution Ave, N.W.
   Washington, DC 20210
ON THE INTERNET:
http://www.doleta.gov/programs/programs.htm

Apprenticeship Training
The Bureau of Apprenticeship and Training registers apprenticeship programs in 23 states. It also assists State Apprenticeship Councils in 27 states, the District of Columbia, Puerto Rico, and the U.S. Virgin Islands. For further information, write or call:

   Bureau of Apprenticeship and Training
   U.S. Department of Labor
   200 Constitution Ave, N.W.
   Washington, DC 20210
PHONE (202) 219-5921
ON THE INTERNET:
http://www.doleta.gov/programs/programs.htm

The Bureau of Labor Statistics has descriptions of working conditions for a wide variety of specific occupational areas. For more information on the Bureau's publications, write to:

   Bureau of Labor Statistics
   Division of Information Services
   2 Massachusetts Avenue, N.E.
   Room 2860
   Washington, DC 20212
Information specialists provide a variety of services by telephone: (202)606-5886.
To send a question by fax, please call (202)606-7890.
ON THE INTERNET: http://stats.bls.gov

Unit 1 PROCESSING OCCUPATIONS

   United Food and Commercial Workers
   International Union, AFL-CIO/CLC
   1775 K Street, N.W.
   Washington, DC 20006
   (202) 223-3111
ON THE INTERNET:
http://www.ufcw.org/home.html

   American Institute of Baking
   1213 Bakers Way
   Manhattan KS 66502
PHONE (913)537-4750
ON THE INTERNET: http://www.aibonline.org
The Institute publishes books and manuals about food processing technology, sanitation, bread making, wheat and flour, and other topics. The American Institute of Baking also publishes the Bakers Way Newsletter.

Aluminum, Brick and Glass Workers
International Union
3362 Hollenberg Drive
Bridgeton, MO 63044:,
OFFICIAL PUBLICATION: ABG Light

American Textile Manufacturers
Institute, Inc.
1801 K St., NW
Suite 900
Washington, DC 20006

Institute of Textile Technology
P.O. Box 391
Charlottesville, VA 22901

REFERENCE BOOK: Kadolph, Sara J. *Textiles.*
New York : Macmillan; 1993.

Unit 2 MACHINE TRADES

The National Tooling and Machining
Association
9300 Livingston Road
Fort Washington, MD 20744
(800) 248-6862
ON THE INTERNET: http://www.ntma.org
Ask about their education programs,
training materials, and publications.

The Tooling and Manufacturing
Association
Attention: Education Department
1177 South Dee Road
Park Ridge, IL 60068

International Association of Machinists
and Aerospace Workers
9000 Machinists Place, Upper Marlboro,
MD 20772-2687
PHONE (301)967-4500
FAX (301)967-4586
ON THE INTERNET: http://www.iamaw.org

The Association for Manufacturing
Technology
7901 Westpark Drive
McLean, VA 22102

Ask about apprenticeship opportunities in
machinery repairs.

For a list of schools offering courses in
vending machine repair, write to:
    National Automatic Merchandising
    Association
    20 North Wacker Drive
    Suite 3500
    Chicago, IL 60606-3102

REFERENCE BOOK: Garvey, Lonny D.
Opportunities in the machine trades
Lincolnwood Ill. : VGM Career Horizons,
1994.

Automotive Service Association, Inc.
1901 Airport Freeway
Bedford TX, 76021-5732

National Automotive Technicians
Education Foundation
13505 Dulles Technology Drive
Herndon, VA 22071-3415
Ask about certified automotive mechanic
training programs.

AMI, Inc., formerly American
Motorcycle Institute
3042 W. International Speedway Blvd.
Daytona Beach, FL 32124
PHONE (800)881-2264
FAX (904)252-3523
ON THE INTERNET:
http://www.amiwrench.com
Ask for information about a career in
motorcycle and watercraft.

Unit 3 STRUCTURAL WORK OCCUPATIONS

United Brotherhood of Carpenters and
Joiners of America
101 Constitution Ave., NW
Washington, DC 20001

Associated Builders and Contractors
1300 North 17th Street
Rosslyn, VA 22209

Associated General Contractors of
America, Inc.
1957 E Street, NW
Washington, DC 20006

Floor Covering Installation Contractors
Association
P. O. Box 948
Dalton GA 30722-0948

REFERENCE BOOK: Garstein, A. S., *The how-to handbook of carpets : a comprehensive guide to retail selling, measuring and estimating, installation, cleaning and maintenance.* New York, Carpet Training Institute, 1979.

Plasterers' and Cement Masons' International Association of the United States and Canada
1125 17th Street, NW
Washington, DC 20036

International Brotherhood of Painters and Allied Trades
1750 New York Ave., NW
Washington, DC 20006

International Union of Bricklayers and Allied Craftsmen
International Masonry Institute
815 15th Street, NW
Washington, DC 20005

International Institute for Lath & Plaster
820 Transfer Road, Suite 34
St. Paul, MN 55114

WALLS & CEILINGS ONLINE: the internet source for information about the walls and ceilings industry
ON THE INTERNET: http://www.wconline.com

Walls & Ceilings Magazine
3702 S. Virginia St. #G12-334
Reno, Nevada 89502
(800)746-4926

UNIT 4 BENCHWORK OCCUPATIONS

American Furniture Manufacturers Association
P. O. Box HP-7
High Point, NC 27261

The American Society Of Furniture Artists (ASOFA)
P.O. Box 35339
Houston, TX 77235
PHONE OR FAX AT: (713)721-7600.
E-MAIL: adam@asofa.org

World Wide Web Sites for Woodworking Associations
http://www.woodworking.com/person.html

Schlage Lock Company, a division of Worldwide Ingersoll-Rand
ON THE INTERNET:
http://www.schlagelock.com/index.html

TRADE MAGAZINE: The National Locksmith
National Publishing Company
ON THE INTERNET:
http://www.TheNationalLocksmith.com/index.htm

REFERENCE BOOKS: Phillips, Bill; The *Complete Book of Locks & Locksmithing,* 4th ed.
McGraw-Hill, Inc. 1995

Phillips, Bill; Professional Locksmithing Techniques, 2nd Edition
TAB Books/McGraw-Hill 1996

Jewelers of America, Inc.
Education Department
1185 Avenue of the Americas
New York, NY 10036
PHONE (212) 768-8777
FAX 768-8087
800 223 0673

Gemological Institute of America
World Headquarters
1660 Stewart Street
Santa Monica, California 90404
PHONE (310) 829-2991
FAX (310) 453-7674
800 421 7250

Gemological Institute of America
580 Fifth Avenue
New York, New York 10036
PHONE (212) 944-5900
FAX (212) 719-9563

REFERENCE BOOK: Jarvis, Charles A.
Jewelery manufacture and repair. London :
N.A.G. Press, 1978.

G L O S S A R Y

access passage; way to get into

adhesives sticky substances used for gluing

alignment arrangement in a straight line

apprenticeship time during which someone is learning a trade

bales large, bound bundles of raw or finished materials

bittings the cuts and jags in the shaft of a key

blank key key without bittings cut in it

blueprints carefully designed plans or technical drawings

boring making a hole in or through a piece of metal by machine tool

buffers materials that polish or shine

canisters large containers for holding liquids

carburetor device for mixing air with fuel in a car's engine

chute slanting passage, down which things are dropped

code letters and numbers in a manual that identify a type of key

combination lock lock that is opened by turning a dial to specified numbers in a certain sequence

contaminate make unclean and not fit for use

contemporary current; modern

conveyor belt continuously moving belt that moves things from one place to another

cubic zirconium lustrous gray-white metallic element used as a substitute for diamonds

cullet recycled waste glass

dough soft, thick mixture of flour and a liquid

drill press machine tool for making holes in metal

emissions substances released into the air

engraved carved or cut into a hard surface

fibers threadlike strands of cotton, wool, or nylon

gauge measurement made according to a certain standard

gauges instruments used for measuring or testing

grinder machine tool for finishing or sharpening metal pieces

grinders materials that shape or refine by using friction

gypsum mineral used in making plaster

impression mark made on the surface of a blank key

ingredients things combined together to form a food

inspect look at carefully for errors

insulated covered with material that limits the passage of heat in or out

insulation materials used to prevent passage of heat or cold

inventory list of supplies on hand including totals

lathe machine tool for cutting and shaping metals

lathing series of thin strips of wood or metal used to support plaster for making walls

lattice open framework made of interwoven strips of wood

linseed oil oil extracted from pressed seeds of the flax plant

lockpick tool that opens a lock

lubricant slippery substance, such as oil, used to coat the surfaces of working parts

lug nuts caps that fit over a bolt

malfunctioning not working correctly

manual book of instructions for employees

manufacturing the making of things by hand or by machine, especially in large amounts

masonry stonework or brickwork

molten melted and hot

nonflammable not likely to catch on fire easily

occupants people who live in a particular place

odometer instrument on the dashboard of a vehicle that measures distance traveled

particle board man-made board made from small pieces of wood that are bonded together

pliers small pinchers for bending, twisting, or holding things

precision exactness; very little error

pressure-treated processed to prevent warping and other damage

priming preparing for painting by applying an undercoat

production the making of something

prototype first model of something, upon which later examples are based

raw natural; not man-made or processed

recalibrate fix, check, or correct measurements again

refrigerant liquid used for cooling

rotating turning or spinning on an axis

roving a strand made up of several slivers

sanitize make clean

shock absorber car part that takes up the impact of bumps on the road

sliver a long, loose rope of yarn

solder torch tool that joins or mends metal parts by melting with heat

spools rods with a rim at each end and a hole through the middle

stains liquids that change the color of wood

standards widely accepted rules

starch a substance that stiffens fabrics and yarns

steering linkage connection between the steering wheel and the tires

stock items on hand for future sale

texture the look or feel of something based on its basic materials

tire pressure amount of compressed air inside a tire

traditional conforming to styles of the past

tumbler cylinder of the lock that holds pins in place

union organization of workers formed to achieve common goals

unsanitary not clean

varnishes colorless, oil-based paints that dry and leave a thin, hard, glossy finish

veneer thin layer of fine wood glued to plywood or particle board to give the look of solid wood

ventilate allow fresh air in

vermiculite mineral used in insulation, made from expanded mica

vibrates moves back and forth rapidly

wire-mesh netting metal screening with holes for holding plaster

yarn raw or man-made fibers twisted into strands

yeast substance that makes baked goods rise, or puff up

INDEX

A N S W E R K E Y

UNIT ONE: PROCESSING OCCUPATIONS

Lesson 1: Working in Food Processing

CHECK YOUR UNDERSTANDING

page 5

  1. b
  2. b
  3. c
  4. d
  5. a

CHECK YOUR UNDERSTANDING

page 8

  1. d
  2. c
  3. b
  4. d

LESSON WRAP-UP

page 9

Your answers may be similar to these samples:

  1. If you know the main idea or basics of a process or task, the details are easier to learn and remember.

  2. The main idea gives a general idea of the passage. The other sentences give more specific information and support the passage.

Lesson 2: Working in Glass Manufacturing

CHECK YOUR UNDERSTANDING

pages 14-15

  1. b
  2. a
  3. a, b, c
  4. a, b, c
  5. a, c, d
  6. b, c, d

CHECK YOUR UNDERSTANDING

page 16

  1. FALSE
  2. FALSE
  3. TRUE
  4. FALSE
  5. FALSE
  6. FALSE
  7. TRUE

LESSON WRAP-UP

page 17

  1. Your details may include: Glass has been made for thousands of years. Molten glass is melted. Cullet is recycled waste glass. Very hot furnaces are needed to make glass.

  2. Your main idea might be: Glass making is a detailed and interesting process.

Lesson 3: Working in Textile Manufacturing

CHECK YOUR UNDERSTANDING

Page 21

  1. 3
  2. Yarn is wound onto large spools by warper operators.
  3. weaving yarn, looping yarn, bonding fibers together
  4. The slasher operator coats the yarn with starch to protect the yarn.
  5. chemicals, heat, and pressure

CHECK YOUR UNDERSTANDING

page 23-24

  1. carding
  2. 5/8 and 5/11
  3. carding
  4. #ER216

5. Your flowchart should look something like this:

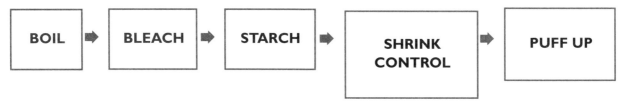

LESSON WRAP-UP
page 25
Here are some sample flowcharts:

1.

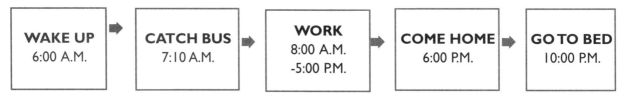

2.

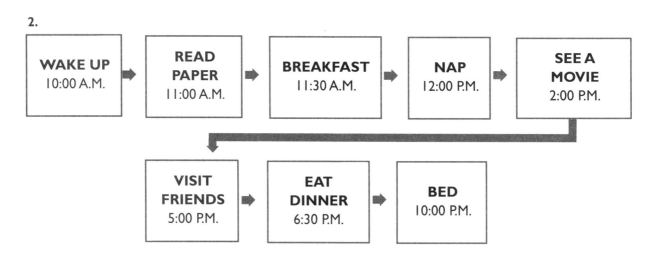

UNIT ONE REVIEW
page 26
Compare your answers to these examples.

1. A main idea is the most important point made in a paragraph or passage. It tells what the other sentences are about. A supporting detail gives more information about the main idea. It helps make the main idea clearer.

2. a. If you don't understand the details on a fire safety poster, you may not know how to escape a burning building.

   b. You need to understand the details of your work contract in order to be sure you are getting paid the amount you should be.

   c. Understanding the details of a customer order is important in making sure customers get what they want.

3. A flowchart is a drawing of a process. With boxes, circles, and arrows, it shows what steps are performed in what order. It is used because it is often easier to follow than a long passage. It can be used as a quick reference.

4. A sample answer might read: Of the jobs, I'd like to be a bakery product worker most. I like the idea of working with food

in a really clean environment. I insist that the food products I buy are fresh and safe, so I know I would take my job seriously. I'd also be interested in seeing those huge amounts of dough!

UNIT TWO: MACHINE TRADES OCCUPATIONS

Lesson 4: Servicing Automobiles

CHECK YOUR UNDERSTANDING

page 32

1. a, d
2. d
3. b, c
4, 5. Compare your cause-and-effect sentences to these:

My Toyota's shock absorber is defective, so the car wheels shake.

Because parts of the steering linkage are worn, the car wheels shake.

Joe's car pulls to the left because its wheels are out of alignment.

The van had incorrect wheel size, so the tires wore unevenly.

CHECK YOUR UNDERSTANDING

pages 34-35

1. A mechanic forgot to put on his gloves when he poured refrigerant, and some splashed on his left hand. As a result, he got frostbite.
2. The refrigerant used at Bob's Station was not kept clean and charged; so when Justin had his car serviced this summer, the air conditioning did not work.
3. There may have been a crack in the air-conditioning fittings.
4. The air-conditioning system in Kim's car failed because the refrigerant was unlabeled and may have been made for other purposes.

LESSON WRAP-UP

page 35

Here are some sample answers:

1. I want to get and keep a good-paying job. Therefore, I'll keep going to classes and improve my skills.
2. If a person is thoughtful, he or she will have lots of good friends.
3. Because reading skills are important on the job, I worked to improve mine.
4. a. Mary yelled at her son. As a result, he cleaned his room.

b. We could not hear the speaker because the crowd was so noisy.

c. I'll buy groceries if I get paid today.

Lesson 5: Working with Machines

CHECK YOUR UNDERSTANDING

page 40

1. shut-down dial and emergency stop button
2. Both methods stop the turning machine.

Both methods do not affect materials.
3. One is a dial; one is a button.

One stops the conveyor belt and rotating arm; the other cuts off electrical power.

One restarts by turning the dial; one does not.
4. however, both, while on the other hand
5. c, d
6. page 47, step 3.1

CHECK YOUR UNDERSTANDING

page 42

1. Highsite Manufacturing is a large plant, whereas Mac's Machine Shop is small.
2. Machinists at Mac's work on a variety of machines; on the other hand, at Highsite, machinists operate the same machine all day.
3. Workers stand all day at Highsite, while at Mac's some work may be done sitting outdoors.
4. Weekly wages at Highsite are about

$50 more than at Mac's, and opportunity for advancement is greater at Highsite.

LESSON WRAP-UP

page 43

Compare your answers to these samples:

1. When two things are being compared and contrasted, the writer is describing what is similar about the things and what is different.

2. Check your diagram against this sample:

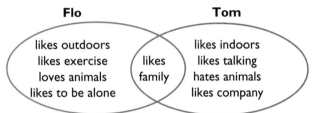

3. Here is the sample paragraph: My sister is very different from my brother, even though they are from the same family. My sister Flo likes to be outdoors a lot. She likes nature and exercise. My brother Tom, however, likes staying inside with plenty of food and conversation. While Flo could spend all of the 4th of July holiday at the beach with no company but her two dogs, Tom (who hates animals) would rather throw a huge party in the rec room with food and entertainment. But in the end, they both like to get together for a quiet evening with their children and grandchildren.

Lesson 6: Servicing Vending Machines

CHECK YOUR UNDERSTANDING

pages 46-47

   1. b

   2. a

   3. a, b

   4. a

CHECK YOUR UNDERSTANDING

page 48

   1. c

   2. b

   3. b

   4. b

LESSON WRAP-UP

page 49

Here are some sample responses:

1. I use a chart each time I look at a nutritional food label. It is easy to understand because you can just scan it for the information you need. For example, I look right at the columns marked "vitamins" and "calories." Then, I can compare this information with the items marked "fats."

2. I would like having a job in vending machine service because I would be working on my own, it might pay well, and it would get me out of the office. The parts of the job that I would dislike are that it is a lot of responsibility, it is physically demanding, and it involves a lot of driving.

UNIT TWO REVIEW

Page 50

Compare your answers to these examples.

1. A vending machine repair person and an auto mechanic both work on machines. They both need to use their hands and many kinds of tools well. They both have to be able to read manuals and work orders. They both have to follow instructions carefully. However, a vending machine repair person probably spends more time going to customer locaions and relating to customers than an auto mechanic does.

2. It's a rainy day: We decided not to go to the beach. The party was moved indoors.

You win a million dollars. You buy a new car for your dad.

You take a long trip with your family.

You stay late at work every day one week. Your supervisor pays you overtime. Your supervisor gives you a day off.

A friend is very sick: You spend a lot of

time helping your friend's family. You spend a lot of time with your friend.

3. A worker might quit a job for a variety of reasons. One reason might be that the pay is too low and another job that pays more becomes available. Or maybe the hours of the job were interfering with family life. A more serious cause for quitting might be some kind of harrassment on the job.

4. A sample answer might read: I would like to be an auto mechanic because I love cars. I think I have a good basic understanding of how cars work, and I'm interested in learning more. The idea of working in a garage and trying to figure out what is wrong with all kinds of cars really appeals to me. Also, I don't mind getting my hands dirty.

UNIT THREE: STRUCTURAL WORK OCCUPATIONS

Lesson 7: Working in Plastering

CHECK YOUR UNDERSTANDING

page 56
1. b
2. a
3. c
4. b
5. a
6. a

CHECK YOUR UNDERSTANDING

page 58
1. b
2. a
3. c

LESSON WRAP-UP

page 59
Here are some suggested answers:
1. a. You need to know how to read to be a plasterer.

Clues: You need to read instructions, labels, orders, memos.

b. Plastering is a safe way to build and can be beautiful.
Clues: Plastering is a way to fireproof; you can make decorative textures and moldings out of plaster.

c. Plastering is not a simple process.
Clues: Plastering requires a variety of materials mixed together the right way; you need to make lathing and use wire-mesh netting; you need to wear stilts to reach high places.

2. A sample answer might read: Once last year, it was snowing incredibly hard and lots of schools and businesses were closing. Because the night shift at my buddy's factory did not have to work, I figured I didn't have to go in either. But my shift was still on, and everybody except me showed up. I should have called to check if my company was open or not.

Lesson 8: Installing Floor Covering

CHECK YOUR UNDERSTANDING

page 64
1. c
2. d
3. a
4. 2, 6, 1, 5, 3, 4

CHECK YOUR UNDERSTANDING

pages 66-67
1. use dry cleaning fluid
2. detergent solution, white vinegar solution, warm water, spot removal kit
3. TRUE
4. No; he should have tried detergent first.

LESSON WRAP-UP

page 67
Here is a sample answer:
To make scrambled eggs, first crack three eggs into a bowl. Be careful not to get any shells in it. Add 1/4 cup of milk. Beat with

a fork or whisk. Add salt and pepper if you like. Set the mixture aside. In a 13" skillet, melt a little butter, or spray with shortening. With the stove on medium-high, pour the egg mixture into the skillet. Let it set for about one minute, and then stir. As the eggs cook, keep stirring and flipping them over. When they have cooked to your liking, use a spatula to transfer them to your plate.

Lesson 9: Working as a Carpenter's Assistant

CHECK YOUR UNDERSTANDING

pages 71-72

1. FALSE
2. b, c, and d
3. TRUE
4. Transportation workers' average wages have been lowered 10 percent.

CHECK YOUR UNDERSTANDING

page 74

1. My neighbor's deck was built in three weeks.

You have been working three weeks, and you are not done yet.

The lattice work that you have installed is 4 feet high.

It is higher than I ordered.

2. You are taking too long to complete the job.

The deck looks too small compared to my neighbor's.

3. YES; the work order states that it should be $3\frac{1}{2}$ feet high.

4. $27\frac{1}{2}$ feet by 15 feet

5. They can measure the deck to make sure it matches the work order.

LESSON WRAP-UP

page 75

Here are some sample answers:

1. You might take a break, and your boss might see you and give you a warning.

2. You might not correct the problem. Then, your supervisor might question why you did not listen to him. He may have to show you how he measured and found the boards too short. He may also give you a warning or deduct something from your paycheck for the waste.

UNIT THREE REVIEW

page 76

Compare your answers to these examples.

1. Last week, I arrived at work, and everyone else was already busy at their desks. It was only 8:05! My supervisor and her supervisor were very dressed up—more so than usual. The conference room was set up with notepads, pens, fresh coffee, and donuts. The atmosphere in the office was very serious compared to the usual joking around. Right then I figured out what must be going on. The company president was coming in for a meeting.

2. If you are walking, go to the end of East St., and take a left onto Bridge St. Keep walking past a Mobil gas station on your left and a church on your right. At the next set of lights, turn right onto Main St. and walk one block. The grocery store is on your right, at the corner of Main St. and Roosevelt Avenue.

3. OPINION: Plastering seems like a really uncomfortable job. All that dust probably irritates your eyes, and the masks you wear can't keep all the dust from getting into your lungs. Plus it seems like a really boring job.

FACT: The job of plasterer requires the ability to work with your hands. It also requires workers to follow directions carefully and pay attention to details. Plastering is mostly indoor work, and there is some bending and lifting involved.

UNIT FOUR: BENCH WORK OCCUPATIONS

Lesson 10: Making Wood Furniture

CHECK YOUR UNDERSTANDING

page 81

1. c
2. b
3. d
4. b

CHECK YOUR UNDERSTANDING

page 84

1. c
2. a
3. c
4. a
5. Buy mahogany. The survey shows that 40 percent of people think mahogany is the most beautiful wood. So, if this mahogany costs no more than pine, you can conclude that you would gain a profit using it for furniture.

6. You can conclude that for most people, furniture is not something to shop for monthly. The furniture company can use this information to plan how much furniture they make in a year.

LESSON WRAP-UP

page 85

1. Here's one example:
* You can work a day shift or a night shift at this job.
* You wear a uniform at this job.
* The job involves being out walking or driving.
* This job involves helping and protecting.
* A weapon is sometimes carried on this job.

Answer: security guard or police officer

2. Here's an example:

Last year I jumped to a conclusion that I should not have. For about two weeks in September, my wife was making a lot of strange phone calls. She'd be talking to someone, but she would hang up when I'd come into the room. Then I'd see her whispering to our two teenage kids. She was always too busy to go out, and it seemed like she was really distracted. So I figured she was going to leave me or something. But what I forgot was that my thirtieth birthday was September 23, and it turned out she had planned a huge surprise party for me!

Lesson 11: Working as a Locksmith

CHECK YOUR UNDERSTANDING

page 90

1. b
2. b, c, d
3. a, d
4. Here is a sample answer: Tom says that they'll earn more money in the future if they spend time and money now. Even though there is no guarantee, I agree with him. It always helps to learn new things. Most people waste part of their week, anyway. It would be better to spend that time improving job skills.

CHECK YOUR UNDERSTANDING

pages 92-93

1. B
2. D
3. E
4. none
5. C

LESSON WRAP-UP

page 93

1. Sample: Lately, I've been having a problem with one of my co-workers. He

talks to me all day long, even when I'm trying to concentrate on something. I've tried to ignore him, but he doesn't get it.

    2. List of possible solutions:
- Speak to the co-worker directly and explain the problem.
- Speak to a supervisor and asked to be moved to a different area.

Lesson 12: Making and Repairing Jewelry

CHECK YOUR UNDERSTANDING
page 96

    1. Explained cleaning and polishing.

    2. Answered customer calls.

    3. Began repairing Mrs. Olsen's chain.

    4. Finished Mrs. Olsen's chain.

    5. Repaired and polished remaining orders.

    6. Repaired Mr. Sullivan's watch.

    7. Began wax mold for opal rings.

    8. Worked on opal ring mold.

    9. Injected sterling silver into mold.

    10. Began setting opals.

    11. Sample: It might be a good idea to evaluate a worker's time in order to get a better idea of how much time is spent on each task and to determine whether additional help is needed—in this case, perhaps for addressing customer concerns

CHECK YOUR UNDERSTANDING
page 98

Suggested responses:

	Advantages	Disadvantages
Costume Jewelry	costs less money; looks like the real thing; can have more of it; doesn't need polishing	breaks easily; can irritate the skin; doesn't increase in value; can become dated
Fine Jewelry	always has value; never ages; increases in value; doesn't break; looks and feels better	expensive

LESSON WRAP-UP
page 99

Suggested responses:

    Group 1: Appearance: large, round, oval, tiny, square, red

    Group 2: Numbers: two, three, four eight, ten

    Group 3: Materials: silver, gold, diamond, ruby, sapphire

Suggested responses for original lists:

    a. Furniture: chairs, tables, beds, chests, desks, lamps

    b. Jewelry: bracelets, pins, necklaces, earrings, rings, watches

    c. Hand tools: wrench, pliers, screwdriver, hammer, plane, ruler

UNIT FOUR REVIEW
page 100

Compare your answers to these examples.

    1. Of the three jobs, I'd least like to be a locksmith. I would not like to have responsibility for so many people's safety. I also can't see well without my glasses, and I don't like doing a lot of close-up detail work. The idea of having to travel around to different job sites does not appeal to me either. I like to work in one place all day.

    2. It seems to me that the most difficult part of being a jewelry maker would be following orders. From the descriptions in this lesson, it's clear that when you work for a large manufacturer, you have to do what you're told—even if you think it doesn't look good. I love jewelry, and I think I'm pretty good with design. It would

be hard for me to make jewelry that I think is unattractive. I'd always want to do my own thing.

3. One possible solution is to talk directly to the workers who were not following safety rules. You could tell them what you saw and how these actions were putting the whole company in danger. Most people are pretty resonable, so this would probably work. If they did not listen, however, another solution would be to report the incident for a supervisor to handle.

4. If information is not organized, jobs get done more slowly. When you have to search around to find facts, customer orders or inventory lists, the process comes to a halt. If, on the other hand, information is organized and easy to find, no time is wasted. Also, if information is not well organized, it's easier to make a mistake on the job.